MIX
Papier aus verantwortungsvollen Quellen
Paper from responsible sources
FSC® C105338

Nicolaas A. Smit

The Evolution of the Responsibility to Protect

From the ICISS to the 2005 World Summit

Anchor Academic Publishing

Smit, Nicolaas A.: The Evolution of the Responsibility to Protect. From the ICISS to the
2005 World Summit. Hamburg, Anchor Academic Publishing 2013

Buch-ISBN: 978-3-95489-130-6
PDF-eBook-ISBN: 978-3-95489-630-1
Druck/Herstellung: Anchor Academic Publishing, Hamburg, 2013

Bibliografische Information der Deutschen Nationalbibliothek:
Die Deutsche Nationalbibliothek verzeichnet diese Publikation in der Deutschen
Nationalbibliografie; detaillierte bibliografische Daten sind im Internet über
http://dnb.d-nb.de abrufbar.

All rights reserved. This publication may not be reproduced, stored in a retrieval system
or transmitted, in any form or by any means, electronic, mechanical, photocopying,
recording or otherwise, without the prior permission of the publishers.

Das Werk einschließlich aller seiner Teile ist urheberrechtlich geschützt. Jede Verwertung
außerhalb der Grenzen des Urheberrechtsgesetzes ist ohne Zustimmung des Verlages
unzulässig und strafbar. Dies gilt insbesondere für Vervielfältigungen, Übersetzungen,
Mikroverfilmungen und die Einspeicherung und Bearbeitung in elektronischen Systemen.

Die Wiedergabe von Gebrauchsnamen, Handelsnamen, Warenbezeichnungen usw. in
diesem Werk berechtigt auch ohne besondere Kennzeichnung nicht zu der Annahme,
dass solche Namen im Sinne der Warenzeichen- und Markenschutz-Gesetzgebung als frei
zu betrachten wären und daher von jedermann benutzt werden dürften.

Die Informationen in diesem Werk wurden mit Sorgfalt erarbeitet. Dennoch können
Fehler nicht vollständig ausgeschlossen werden und der Diplomica Verlag, die Autoren
oder Übersetzer übernehmen keine juristische Verantwortung oder irgendeine Haftung
für evtl. verbliebene fehlerhafte Angaben und deren Folgen.

Alle Rechte vorbehalten

© Anchor Academic Publishing, Imprint der Diplomica Verlag GmbH
Hermannstal 119k, 22119 Hamburg
http://www.diplomica-verlag.de, Hamburg 2013
Printed in Germany

Table of Contents

Chapter 1 1

Chapter 2 4

Chapter 3 13

Chapter 4 32

Chapter 5 42

References 45

List of Acronyms

African Union:	A.U.
United Nations:	U.N.
International Commission on Intervention and State Sovereignty:	ICISS
Permanent Five United Nations Security Council Members:	P-5
Responsibility to Protect	R2P
High Level Panel on Threats, Challenges and Change:	HLP
United States:	U.S.
United Kingdom:	U.K.
Foreign Direct Investment:	FDI
United Nations Economic and Social Council:	UCOSOC
United Nations Assistance Mission in Rwanda:	UNAMIR
United Nations Protection Force for the Former Yugoslavia:	UNPROFOR
United Nations High Commissioner for Refugees:	UNHCR
International Committee of the Red Cross:	ICRC
Internally Displaced Persons:	IDP
Economic Community of West African States:	ECOWAS
Economic Community of West African States Monitoring Group:	ECOMOG
European Union:	E.U.
Weapons of Mass Destruction:	WMD

Chapter 1

The International Commission on Intervention and State Sovereignty (ICISS) published its report, *The Responsibility to Protect*, (hereafter referred to as the Report) in 2001.[1] The Report followed the 9/11 attacks on the World Trade Centre and the Pentagon, and the subsequent US-led war on terror has largely overshadowed the debate on humanitarian intervention which the Report aimed to reignite.[2] The Report has, however, provided answers to issues that were central to the debate surrounding humanitarian intervention during the 1990s, namely, just cause, right authority and the balance between the protection of human rights and sovereignty, but has in the process sparked a new debate centring around the principle it introduced, that of the Responsibility to Protect (R2P). The establishment of the ICISS and the subsequent publication of its report were in response to a challenge laid down by then Secretary-General of the United Nations (U.N.) Kofi Annan:

> If humanitarian intervention is indeed an unacceptable assault on sovereignty, how should we respond to a Rwanda, to a Srebrenica – to gross and systematic violations of human rights that offend every precept of common humanity?[3]

The Canadian government, acting on the initiative and ingenuity of Foreign Minister Lloyd Axworthy,[4] created an international commission which was tasked to "wrestle with the whole range of questions – legal, moral, operational and political – rolled up in this debate, to consult with the widest range of opinion around the world, and to bring back a report that would help the Secretary-General and everyone else find some new common ground."[5] The Report envisions a re-conceptualisation of sovereignty, adding to it a fourth dimension, namely that sovereignty involves a threefold responsibility of states.[6] This re-conceptualisation does not amount to a dilution or transfer of state sovereignty, but rather, a "necessary-re-characterisation ...from *sovereignty as control* to *sovereignty as responsibility* in both internal functions and external duties."[7] The Report's central theme is the notion that states are responsible for the protection and well-being of their citizens, but where a state is either

---

[1] Alex J. Bellamy, *Responsibility to Protect* (Cambridge: Polity Press, 2009), 51; Gareth Evans, The Responsibility to Protect: Ending Mass Atrocity Crimes Once and for All (Washington D.C.: The Brookings Institution, 2008), 31.
[2] Evans, *The Responsibility to Protect*, 44; D. O. Quinn, "The Responsibility to Protect" (MA diss., Canadian Forces College, 2007), 50.
[3] Kofi Annan, Millennium Report of the Secretary General of the United Nations (New York: United Nations Department of Public Information, 2000), 48.
[4] Evans, *The Responsibility to Protect*, 38.
[5] The International Commission on Intervention and State Sovereignty (ICISS), *The Responsibility to Protect* (Ottawa: International Development Research Centre, 2001), vii.
[6] ICISS, 13; Nick Grono, "Briefing – Darfur: The Inrenational Community's Failure to Protect," *African Affairs* 105 (2006): 623; Paul D. Williams and Alex J. Bellamy, "The Responsibility to Protect and the Crisis in Darfur," Security Dialogue 36 (2005): 28.
[7] ICISS, 13

unable or unwilling to discharge this responsibility, it is then transferred to the international community.[8] Rather than contradictory – as was suggested in the previous debate – the Report asserts that the relationship between intervention on the basis of human rights and sovereignty is complementary.[9]

From its inception in 2001, the principle of R2P? has progressed to worldwide acceptance remarkably fast, as it was widely accepted by the international community at the 2005 World Summit.[10] As endorsed at the 2005 World Summit, the R2P is significantly different from its articulation in the ICISS report.[11] A large portion of the literature dealing with the evolution of the R2P focuses on the principle's progression from the ICISS report to the HLP report, the Secretary-General's report and ultimately the 2005 World Summit Outcome Document. This thesis aims to provide a discussion of the main factors influencing the debate around the R2P and the principle's evolution, namely, the war on terror and the 2003 war in Iraq, the crisis in Darfur, and lastly, U.N. Security Council buy-in regarding the ICISS articulated criteria to guide the use of military force in humanitarian intervention. Toward this end, a background to humanitarian intervention is provided, from which the focus shifts to a discussion of the ICISS and the R2P. Finally, the magnifying glass is cast on the version of R2P as articulated in the World Summit outcome document and the most significant events and arguments that have informed the debate around the R2P, and the emergence of what is termed 'R2P Lite'. The manner in which the U.S. has pursued the war on terror, the waging of war in Iraq (2003), and the use of humanitarian justification to legitimise that war, has been a significant factor influencing the debate around R2P.[12] Using the debates on humanitarian intervention in Darfur as a reference point, an argument can be made that the war in Iraq has "undermined the standing of the United States and the U.K as norm carriers."[13] Furthermore, an argument can be made that an underlying theme in the

---

[8] Alex J. Bellamy, "Responsibility to Protect or Trojan Horse? The Crisis in Darfur and Humanitarian Intervention After Iraq," *Ethics and International Affairs* 19 (2005): 35; Christina G. Badescu and Linnea Bergholm, "The Responsibility to Protect and the Conflict in Darfur: The Big Let-Down," *Security Dialogue* 40 (2009): 288, 290; Williams and Bellamy, 28.
[9] S. Neil Macfarlane, Carolin J. Thielking and Thomas G. Weiss, "*The Responsibility to Protect*: Is Anyone Interested in Humanitarian Intervention?" *Third World Quarterly* 25 (2004): 978; Quinn, 34.
[10] Alicia Bannon, "The Responsibility to Protect: The U.N. World Summit and the Question of Unilateralism," *The Yale Law Journal* 115 (2006): 1158-9; Grono, 622; 2005 World Summit, Sept. 14-16, 2005, *2005 World Summit Outcome*, 138-9, U.N. Doc. A/60/L.1 (Sept. 20, 2005); Mahmood Mamdani, "Responsibility to Protect or Right to Punish," *Journal of Intervention and Stabilising* 4 (2010): 55.
[11] Bellamy, *Responsibility to Protect*, 83.
[12] Thomas G. Weiss, "R2P After 9/11 and the World Summit," *Wisconsin International Law Journal* 24 (2006): 748; Williams and Bellamy, *Responsibility to Protect*, 36-7; Gareth Evans, "From Humanitarian Intervention to the Responsibility to Protect," *Wisconsin International Law Journal* 24(2006): 717.
[13] Bellamy, *Trojan Horse*, 32.

evolution of the R2P, and the reason for this thesis, is that we are currently experiencing a changing of the writers of the rules of the international system.[14]

Alex Bellamy argues that the main activists of humanitarian intervention have suffered a "credibility crisis," with the real danger being that appeals to a R2P "will evaporate amid disputes about where that responsibility lies."[15] Initially my understanding was that with regards to the 2003 crisis in Darfur, R2P as a principle had failed to live up to the standards that it set, and that this failure was the primary reason behind the international community's response (or rather lack thereof). However, what I have come to discover was that by introducing the "language of a 'responsibility to protect'," into the debates around Darfur, has enabled those who are opposed to intervention "to legitimise arguments against action"[16] by claiming that in a number of disputed cases the primary responsibility remains with the state in question and has yet not been transferred to the international community.[17] This of course returns the issue to the question of the balance between sovereignty and the protection of human rights, and although the Report stresses that these two aspects are complementary, as is mentioned above. It is apparent that this is an issue of contention not only in the debates surrounding Darfur, but also in the evolution of the R2P, and as such, will receive special attention here, but also because this issue speaks to what is one of the central principles of the international system, namely that of sovereignty as well as the accompanying norm of non-intervention.

---
[14] Ibid.
[15] Ibid, 33.
[16] Ibid, 33.
[17] Ibid, 33.

Chapter 2

This chapter aims to provide a background to humanitarian intervention in order to provide a basis from which to judge the significance of the Report, as well as the concepts and the ideas that it introduced. Furthermore, a central theme of this chapter is the contentious nature of humanitarian intervention, something which has had important implications in the debate around R2P, as well as the principle's evolution. Toward this end, this chapter provides a discussion on the definition and meaning of intervention, from where the focus will shift to the concept of humanitarian intervention. The third part of the chapter deals with intervention (including military) and the U.N. Charter, discussing firstly the argument that humanitarian intervention is legal, and secondly, suggesting that it is illegal.

Intervention refers to a range of non-consensual actions, which is often believed to "challenge the principle of state sovereignty"[18] directly, or as Wheeler and Bellamy define it "in terms of a coercive breach of the walls of the castle of sovereignty."[19] The term's actual meaning can be drawn from the contexts within which it occurs, as well as the purposes for which it is undertaken.[20] Where a target state provides unqualified consent or makes a genuine request, actions are not considered intervention, and consent, if it is to be legally valid, "should emanate from the legal government of a sovereign state and be freely given."[21] Furthermore, any means of interference that does not result in coercion in the domestic affairs of a particular state is not considered intervention.[22] In fact, a primary objective of foreign policy is to persuade both hostile and friendly states alike, to undertake changes in behaviour that are in line with foreign policy goals.[23] Such a definition of intervention is of course not exhaustive, as broader definitions of the term have always been in existence. For instance, in the contemporary era where the international system is characterised by asymmetrical power relations, foreign direct investment (FDI) and economic activities are perceived by some as forms of 'intervention'.[24]

Because the issue of consent has been identified here as one criterion for determining what is considered intervention and what is not, a brief return to it is warranted here. There are some grey areas with regard to consent, and which relate to both military and economic

---

[18] International Commission on Intervention and State Sovereignty (ICISS), *"The Responsibility to Protect: Research Bibliography, Background* (Ottawa: International Development Research Centre, 2001), 15.
[19] Nicholas J. Wheeler and Alex J. Bellamy, "Humanitarian Intervention in World Politics," in *The Globalization of World Politics: An Introduction to International Relations*, eds. John Baylis and Steve Smith (Oxford: Oxford University Press, 2005), 557.
[20] ICISS, *Research Bibliography, Background,* 16.
[21] Ibid.
[22] Ibid.
[23] Ibid.
[24] Ibid.

measures.[25] In some instances the call for military intervention from the target state potentially involves "so much arm-twisting, including economic pressure from Washington-based financial institutions, as to effectively constitute coercion."[26] A number of terms have emerged in thinking about what constitutes coerced consent, including that of 'coercive inducement', and towards ensuring that the request for intervention is not in fact spurious, rather than frame the term merely as a lack of consent, conceptualising it "as a matter of factual intrusiveness"[27] may go some way towards achieving this objective. For a number of definitions of intervention, rather than see consent as an absolute concept, it may be more useful to think of it as a continuum.[28] There is no doubt that the non-consensual use of military force against another state amounts to intervention, but similarly so too is the utilization of non-military measures such as economic and political sanctions, international criminal prosecution and arms embargoes.[29] "Intervention is a concept with a distinct character. This character lies in the use of "forcible" or "non-forcible" measures against a state, without its consent, solely on account of its internal or external behaviour."[30] Although the most frequent end to which intervention has been employed is the protection and safeguarding of significant interests of the intervening state(s), the justification of intervention on the basis of human suffering has a long history, and will be discussed in the following section, I believe it prudent to end this section with R. J. Vincent's definition of intervention:

> Activity undertaken by a state, a group within a state, a group of states or an international organization which interferes coercively in the domestic affairs of another state. It is a discrete event having a beginning and an end, and it is aimed at the authority structure of the target state. It is not necessarily lawful or unlawful, but it does break a conventional pattern of international relations.[31]

The roots of the notion of humanitarian intervention by foreign states following the failure of a state to discharge its responsibility to its citizens can be traced to Hugo Grotius, writing in the 16th Century.[32] Grotius asserted that a foreign state could support the citizens of another state in instances where the target state is engaged in repression of its citizens, who are in turn engaged in legitimate resistance to such repression.[33] However, it is only after 1840 that the first references to humanitarian intervention emerged in international legal writing,

---

[25] Ibid.
[26] Ibid.
[27] Ibid.
[28] Ibid.
[29] Ibid.
[30] Ibid.
[31] R. J. Vincent, *Nonintervention and International Order* (Princeton, NJ: Princeton University Press, 1974), 13, quoted in Nicholas J. Wheeler and Alex J. Bellamy, "Humanitarian Intervention in World Politics," In *The Globalization of World Politics: An Introduction to International Relations*, eds. John Baylis and Steve Smith (Oxford: Oxford University Press, 2005), 557.
[32] Quinn, 6.
[33] Ibid.

and two interventions stand out as primarily responsible for this.[34] The first was the 1827 British, French and Russian intervention in Greece to avert Turkish massacres and halt the suppression of peoples with ties to insurgents, and the second was the 1860 French intervention in Syria aimed at the protection of Maronite Christians.[35] From the period 1827 – 1906, there were no fewer than five "prominent interventions undertaken by European powers against the Ottoman Empire,"[36] and by the second decade of the 20th Century, the rationale underlying intervention had widened to "include the protection of nationals living abroad."[37]

State abuse of sovereignty by cruel and brutal treatment of those within the ambit of its power, be those nationals or non-nationals was the primary cause for calls for intervention.[38] States that engaged in such behaviour were perceived as having opened the door to action by any foreign state or group of states that were willing to intervene. Ellery Stowell illustrates humanitarian intervention thus: "the reliance on force for the justifiable purpose of protecting the inhabitants of another state from the treatment which is so arbitrary and persistently abusive as to exceed the limits of that authority within which the sovereign is presumed to act with reason and justice."[39] However, intervention has and continues to be approached and regarded with suspicion, as many have cast a doubtful eye over the earliest instances of humanitarian intervention. Critics of humanitarian intervention assert that given the lack of an impartial and unbiased mechanism by which to determine when humanitarian intervention is permissible, states are likely to employ humanitarian justifications and motives as a pretext to veil the pursuit of political, economic or strategic interests.[40] This argument has been extended and those who find credence with this line of reasoning claim that humanitarian intervention will become a weapon of the strong employed against the weak.[41] Furthermore, it is doubtless that even when in situations where the goals were less questionable, "the paternalism of intervening powers – which were self appointed custodians of morality and human conscience, as well as the guarantors of international order and security – undermined the credibility of the enterprise."[42]

---

[34] ICISS, *Research Bibliography, Background,* 16.
[35] Ibid.
[36] Ibid.
[37] Ibid.
[38] Ibid, 17.
[39] Ellery Stowell, Intervention in International Law (Washington, DC: J. Byrne, 1921), 53, quoted in International Commission on Intervention and State Sovereignty (ICISS), *"The Responsibility to Protect: Research Bibliography, Background* (Ottawa: International Development Research Centre, 2001), 17.
[40] ICISS, *Research Bibliography, Background,* 17; Wheeler and Bellamy, 558.
[41] Wheeler and Bellamy, 558.
[42] ICISS, *Research Bibliography, Background,* 17.

By the end of the nineteenth century a large number of legal scholars believed "that a doctrine of humanitarian intervention existed in customary international law,"[43] although this claim was disputed to a significant degree. The significance of these conclusions are contested, with some legal scholars arguing that such a doctrine was undoubtedly established in pre-Charter state practice before 1945,[44] "and that it is the parameters, not the existence, of the doctrine that are open to debate."[45] This claim is of course rejected, with other scholars pointing firstly to state practice pre-1945, and the lack of support therein for a "right of humanitarian intervention,"[46] and secondly, citing inconsistency in state practice, especially in the twentieth century.[47] What is evident is that this idea of intervention underwent substantial evolution prior to the emergence of an international system equipped with mechanisms and institutions tasked with the protection of human rights and maintenance of international order.

The definition of humanitarian intervention given above is somewhat dated, and Kenneth Roth provides a definition thereof that is very much in line with that provided for intervention above, namely, "military intervention without the consent of the government whose territory is being invaded,"[48] but qualifies this by stating that only "the imperative of stopping ongoing or imminent mass slaughter might justify the risk to life."[49] Fernando Tesón provides a definition of humanitarian intervention that omits the issue of consent, depicting it as "proportionate help, including forcible help, provided by governments (individually or in alliances) to individuals in another state who are victims of severe tyranny (denial of human rights by their own government) or anarchy (denial of human rights by collapse of social order)."[50]

What these authors share in terms of their understanding of humanitarian intervention, is that both subscribe to a set of principles that either guide or justify/legitimate humanitarian intervention. Roth identifies five factors which, once the abovementioned threshold is met, determine whether military action can be labelled as humanitarian. First, the resort to military force must be "the last reasonable option."[51] Secondly, the primary motive or purpose driving the intervention must necessarily be humanitarian.[52] Third, the intervention must be carried out with the outmost respect for international humanitarian law and human rights, fourth, it must not cause more harm than good, and finally, the intervention "should ideally, though not

---

[43] ICISS, *Research Bibliography, Background*, 17; Wheeler and Bellamy, 558.
[44] ICISS, *Research Bibliography, Background*, 17; Wheeler and Bellamy, 558.
[45] ICISS, *Research Bibliography, Background*, 17.
[46] Wheeler and Bellamy, 558.
[47] ICISS, *Research Bibliography, Background*, 17.
[48] Kenneth Roth, "Was the Iraq War a Humanitarian Intervention?" *Journal of Military Ethics* 5 (2006): 85.
[49] Ibid.
[50] Fernando R. Tesón, "Ending Tyranny in Iraq," *Ethics & International Affairs* 19 (2005): 2.
[51] Roth, 85.
[52] Ibid.

necessarily be endorsed by the U.N. Security Council or another body with significant multilateral authority."[53] Tesón on the other hand provides five principles which are intended to guide humanitarian interventions; firstly, putting an end to anarchy or tyranny must be the aim to which justifiable intervention is directed.[54] Secondly, the doctrine of double effect – "the permissibility of causing serious harm as a side effect of promoting some good end, coupled with an adequate theory of costs and benefits"[55]- apply to and govern humanitarian intervention, as it does all wars. Third, in general terms, it is only the most severe cases of tyranny or anarchy that satisfy the call for humanitarian intervention.[56] Fourth, the intervention must be welcomed by the victims of anarchy,[57] and finally, "humanitarian intervention should preferably receive the approval or support of the community of democratic states."[58] Thus, although these two authors differ on the precise principles to guide humanitarian intervention, these examples are provided to illustrate the evolution of the concept. What this also shows is that one will be hard pressed to find a uniform definition of humanitarian intervention, that the principles guiding it are likely to overlap but will have some divergence, and that humanitarian intervention remains a contentious issue in the international system.

The 20th Century restriction on the "use of force in intervention"[59] can be traced to the Peace of Westphalia, concluded in 1648.[60] Furthermore, the initial "restrictions on recourse to war"[61] were envisioned in the 1928 Kellog-Briand Pact, and the system later crystallized into its contemporary form, as expressed in the U.N. Charter. The threat or actual "use of force against the territorial integrity and political independence of states"[62] has since 1945 been prohibited under the U.N. Charter's Article 2 (4), which grants exception "for the collective use of force under Chapter VII,"[63] and for collective or individual self-defence in a situation of an armed attack under Article 51.[64] Despite the fact that the prohibition on the use of force appears explicitly clear, questions regarding the legality of humanitarian intervention, as for instance in 1946, a prominent legal scholar continued his argument that intervention is permissible by law when a "state is guilty of cruelties against its nationals in a way that denied

---

[53] Ibid, 85-6.
[54] Tesón, 2.
[55] Ibid, 2-3.
[56] Ibid, 3.
[57] Ibid, 3.
[58] Ibid, 3.
[59] Quinn, 6.
[60] Ibid.
[61] ICISS, *Research, Bibliography, Background*, 17.
[62] Ibid.
[63] Ibid.
[64] Ibid.

their fundamental human rights and shocked the conscience of humankind."[65] However, with regard to the forceful intervention by a state or group of states aimed at the protection of "the citizens of another state, the Charter is silent."[66]

Turning to the question of whether or not humanitarian intervention is legal in terms of the U.N. Charter, there are two opposing points of view on this issue. Firstly, there are those who assert that not only is humanitarian intervention legal, but it is also legitimate.[67] These proponents of humanitarian intervention "frequently cite the purposes of the *UN Charter*."[68] Article 1(3) of the Charter states that an explicit function of the U.N. relates to the achievement of international co-operation in the promotion and encouragement of respect for fundamental freedoms and human rights for all, irrespective of sex, religion, language or race. Furthermore, the preamble to the Charter "reaffirm[s] faith in fundamental human rights."[69] Article 13(1)(b) affords the General Assembly the authority and power to facilitate the achievement and fulfilment of human rights, and Article 55(c) requests that the U.N. promote "universal respect for, and observance of, human rights and fundamental freedoms."[70] Article 62(2) affords the Economic and Social Council (ECOSOC) the power and authority to "make recommendations for the purpose of promoting respect for, and observance of, human rights and fundamental freedoms for all,"[71] and Article 68 empowers the Council to establish commissions for the promotion and advancement of human rights.[72] Although these provisions are not a comprehensive list of all the articles of the U.N. Charter that are concerned with the protection of human rights, it is nonetheless clear from the abovementioned articles that the promotion and advancement of human rights are a central concern of the U.N. Charter. Furthermore, the argument can undoubtedly be made that in certain instances "humanitarian intervention is consistent with the objectives of the U.N. Charter."[73]

Article 2(4) of the U.N. Charter emphasises the prohibition of the use or threat of force "against the territorial integrity or political independence of any state."[74] Regarding political independence and territorial integrity, it is arguable that an authentic humanitarian

---

[65] Ibid.
[66] Quinn, 7.
[67] Ronli Sifris, "Operation Iraqi Freedom: United States v Iraq – The Legality of the War," *Melbourne Journal of International Law* 4 (2003): 29.
[68] Ibid.
[69] "Charter of the United Nations," The United Nations (U.N.), accessed October 2, 2010, http://www.un.org/en/documents/charter/preamble.shtml
[70] Ibid, http://www.un.org/en/documents/charter/chapter9.shtml
[71] Ibid, http://www.un.org/en/documents/charter/chapter10.shtml
[72] Ibid.
[73] Sifris, 30.
[74] U.N., http://www.un.org/en/documents/charter/chapter1.shtml

intervention results in neither political subjugation nor territorial conquest.[75] Firstly, the rule asserts that the territorial integrity of a state must be protected from the use of force by another, meaning that "a state's territory must be kept integral – that is, no parts of it may be forcibly separated and given over to another state."[76] Thus, provided that the territorial boundaries of the state in question remain intact, the argument can be made that humanitarian intervention does not amount to a breach of Article 2(4).[77] If one perceives the political independence of a given state as referring to the "right of the people of a state to political independence,"[78] then humanitarian intervention directed towards the protection of the people "would affirm the state's political independence, rather than violate it."[79] This view has been extrapolated and the conclusion has been drawn that even in the event that the government of the state in question is overthrown, its political independence is left unthreatened,[80] as through its oppression of its citizens, the government is perceived as having suffered a loss of legitimacy.[81]

Turning to the argument that humanitarian intervention is illegal; the approach which asserts that humanitarian intervention is in fact legal is a claim which appeals to an individual's sense of compassion and justice.[82] However, an argument can be made "that such an approach does not accord with a commonsense construction of the *UN Charter*."[83] Whereas humanitarian intervention is not explicitly mentioned in the Charter,[84] the notion of sovereignty and the norm of non-intervention that flows from it are clearly articulated by the Charter. Two provisions of the Charter cast doubt over whether "forcible self-help to protect human rights"[85] remains acceptable in terms of international law. Firstly, in terms of Article 2(4) of the Charter, all states reject "the threat or use of force against the territorial integrity or political independence of any state,"[86] which is qualified by the provision relating to self-defence which is contained in Article 51. In the second instance, Article 2(7) prohibits U.N. intervention "in matters which are essentially within the domestic jurisdiction of any state,"[87]

---

[75] Sifris, 30.
[76] Anthony D'Amato, "There is No Norm of Intervention or Non-Intervention in International Law," *International Legal Theory* 7 (2001): 39.
[77] Sifris, 30.
[78] Ibid.
[79] Ibid.
[80] Ibid.
[81] Ibid.
[82] Ibid.
[83] Ibd.
[84] Sifris, 30; Quinn, 7.
[85] Richard Lillich, "Intervention to Protect Human Rights," *McGill Law Journal* 15 (1969): 205, quoted in Ronli Sifris, "Operation Iraqi Freedom: United States v Iraq – The Legality of the War," *Melbourne Journal of International Law* 4 (2003): 31.
[86] U.N., http://www.un.org/en/documents/charter/chapter1.shtml
[87] Ibid.

excluding instances which call for the "application of enforcement measures under Chapter VII."[88]

Article 2(4) essentially serves as a limitation on the use of force, and in fact, "the *travaux preparatoires* suggest that art 2(4) was intended to operate as an absolute prohibition on the use of force."[89] Thus it is exceedingly doubtful if humanitarian intervention has been able to survive the prohibition on the use of force contained in the U.N. Charter. As a result, any reading of Article 2(4), should be done in a context such as this, and should not be subjected to manipulation so as to "reveal an exception to the prohibition that is not evident from a plain reading of the words."[90] The term 'political independence' is broad in scope, and the ordinary meaning thereof not only refers to the government of a state, but embraces the state's sovereignty, dignity and integrity.[91] Similarly, the term 'territorial integrity' is not limited in the sense that it not only refers only to ensuring that no part of the state's territory is separated, but encompasses the territorial inviolability, integrity and sovereignty of the state.[92] As a matter of fact, the *travaux preparatoires* point out that terms such as 'territorial integrity' were included in Article 2(4) as a means to "close all potential loopholes in its prohibition on the use of force, rather than to open new ones."[93] Furthermore, the Charter's preamble confirms the U.N.'s obligation "to save succeeding generations from the scourge of war,"[94] and Article 1(1) explicitly states that a function of the U.N. is the maintenance of "international peace and security."[95] Although the protection and advancement of human rights is a primary objective of the U.N., it does not take precedence over the purpose of restricting the resort to force. Thus, however vital and essential the self determination of peoples and respect for human rights may be, within the U.N. system which is governed by the Charter, it may never jeopardize peace.[96] As a result, it appears as though the U.N. Charter places a prohibition on humanitarian intervention in the absence of a "Security Council resolution authorising the use of force."[97]

---

[88] Richard Lillich, "Intervention to Protect Human Rights," *McGill Law Journal* 15 (1969): 211, quoted in Ronli Sifris, "Operation Iraqi Freedom: United States v Iraq – The Legality of the War," *Melbourne Journal of International Law* 4 (2003): 31.
[89] Sifris, 31.
[90] Ibid.
[91] Ibid.
[92] Ibid.
[93] Jonathan Charney, "Editorial Comments: NATO's Kosovo Intervention – Anticipatory Humanitarian Intervention in Kosovo," *American Journal of International Law* 93 (1993):834, quoted in Ronli Sifris, "Operation Iraqi Freedom: United States v Iraq – The Legality of the War," *Melbourne Journal of International Law* 4 (2003): 31.
[94] U.N., http://www.un.org/en/documents/charter/preamble.shtml
[95] Ibid, http://www.un.org/en/documents/charter/chapter1.shtml
[96] Sifris, 31.
[97] Ibid.

This chapter has aimed to provide a conceptual background to humanitarian intervention, firstly by looking at the meaning and definition of intervention, and also providing two baseline characteristics for what constitutes intervention, namely the use of force, and that the action is carried out without the consent of the target state.[98] Secondly, the chapter has focused on the concept of humanitarian intervention, discussing the roots of the concept, the possibility of a common law right of humanitarian intervention as well as a definition of the concept. Along with this definition, two more contemporary definitions of humanitarian intervention are provided, and the principles that either guide humanitarian intervention,[99] or which are used to determine whether the use of military force can be seen as humanitarian,[100] are also discussed. The final section of the chapter shifts emphasis to humanitarian intervention and the U.N. Charter, taking as its starting point the Charter's restriction on the use of force, providing the basis for the discussion centring on the legality of humanitarian intervention. Here, arguments made for the legality and illegality of humanitarian intervention are discussed. An underlying theme of this chapter has been the contentious nature of humanitarian intervention. This is significant for our purposes as R2P has been approached with the same degree of suspicion as humanitarian intervention, as many prevailing attitudes towards humanitarian intervention have transpired into the debate around R2P and have without doubt influenced the evolution of the principle.

---

[98] ICISS, *Responsibility to Protect*, 15; Wheeler and Bellamy, 557.
[99] Tesón, 2.
[100] Roth, 85.

Chapter 3

The preceding chapter has provided a background to humanitarian intervention to provide, as has been mentioned, a basis from which to assess the significance of the ICISS report as well as the concepts and ideas which it introduced. In this chapter the focus shifts to the ICISS and the R2P, the starting point being a brief discussion of prominent cases where humanitarian intervention has failed, the challenge laid down by the U.N. Secretary-General in response to these failures and the establishment of the ICISS. The second and third parts of this chapter focus on the concept of sovereignty, the initial understanding thereof and its re-conceptualisation. From there the discussion shifts to the core principles and elements of R2P, and the fifth part of the chapter focuses on the just cause thresholds and criteria for legitimacy as articulated in the Report. The final section discusses the difference between R2P and humanitarian intervention.

With regards to past instances of mass human slaughter where the response by the U.N. and the international community to the violence has been insufficient to stop or avert the violence, two prominent cases come to mind, the Rwandan genocide of 1994, and the Srebrenica massacre of 1995; and each will be briefly discussed. With regards to Rwanda, following the assassination of President Juvénal Habyarimana, a "pre-planned strategy of genocide was put into effect,"[101] as Hutu extremists – known as the *Interhamwe* and *Impuzamigambi* – systematically murdered thousands (the highest estimate puts the number of dead at 800 000) of Tutsis, as well as moderate Hutu, over a period of 100 days.[102] At the time of the Rwandan president's death, a U.N. peacekeeping force, 2 500 strong, was stationed in that country under UNAMIR (U.N. Assistance Mission in Rwanda), to monitor and oversee the implementation of the Arusha Accords.[103] However, after the killing of 10 Belgian soldiers, and the stated intention of the Belgian government to withdraw its troop contingent,[104] U.N. Resolution 912 (1994) which contained the Security Council's decision to adjust UNAMIR's mandate, was passed.[105] The Council voted for a reduction in size of the U.N.'s commitment (to 270) on the 21st of April 1994, and the withdrawal of force, as the killing gained momentum, sent an unmistakable signal to the perpetrators of the genocide "that there was little or no international

---

[101] ICISS, *Research, Bibliography, Background*, 97.
[102] ICISS, *Research, Bibliography, Background*, 98; Col. Scott R. Feil, "Could 5,000 Peacekeepers Have Saved 500, 000 Rwandans?: Early Intervention Reconsidered," *Institute for the Study of Diplomacy* 3 (1997): 1; The U.N., "Report of the Independent Inquiry into the Actions of the United Nations During the 1994 Genocide in Rwanda," U.N. Doc. S/1999/1257 (December 15, 1999), 3.
[103] ICISS, *Research, Bibliography, Background*, 97; Feil, 1.
[104] ICISS, *Research, Bibliography, Background*, 98; Feil, 1.
[105] ICISS, *Research, Bibliography, Background*, 98.

resolve to stand in their way."[106] Major General Romeo Dallaire, force commander of UNAMIR, pleaded with the U.N. for 5 000 soldiers, and requested that the rules of engagement be expanded to include civilian protection. However, neither of these requests were approved.[107] The U.N. continued to dither in its response to the horrors unfolding in Rwanda. During the latter stages of April 1994, the Secretary General outlined three possible courses of action to the Security Council: (i) increase the strength of UNAMIR considerably, (ii) reduce the mission's strength, and (iii) withdraw completely.[108] Of the three alternatives, the Secretary-General supported the plan which called for the deployment of 5 500 soldiers to Kigali, and an expanded mandate for UNAMIR.[109] This plan met with opposition from the US, and on the 17th of May 1994 Resolution 918 (1994) was adopted by the Security Council, imposing an arms embargo and authorising UNAMIR's expansion.[110] However, it was only on the 8th of June 1994 that, by adopting Resolution 925 (1994), the Security Council noted with severe distress the reports revealing that acts constituting genocide had been carried out in Rwanda.[111] In a letter dated 20 June 1994, which was addressed to the Secretary-General, France declared its willingness to intervene in Rwanda,[112] and Resolution 929 (1994) was adopted by the Council on the 22nd of June 1994.[113] The Security Council "authorized France to conduct an operation under national command and to control to improve security and protect displaced persons, refugees, and civilians at risk,"[114] and to achieve these objectives by any means necessary.[115]

The Independent Inquiry into the actions of the U.N. during the Rwandan genocide found that the response of the U.N. both before and during the genocide in Rwanda "failed in a number of fundamental respects."[116] The Independent Inquiry identified the overriding failure of the U.N.'s response as "the lack of capacity of the United Nations peacekeeping mission in place to deal with the realities of the challenge it was faced with."[117] The Inquiry identified other failures and mistakes such as the inadequacy of the UNAMIR mandate, the implementation thereof, confusion regarding the rules of engagement, and a "failure to

---

[106] Ibid.
[107] ICISS, *Research, Bibliography, Background*, 98; Feil, 2.
[108] ICISS, *Research, Bibliography, Background*, 98.
[109] Ibid.
[110] Ibid.
[111] Ibid.
[112] ICISS, *Research, Bibliography, Background*, 100; U.N., *Report of the Independent Inquiry*, 27.
[113] ICISS, *Research, Bibliography, Background*, 100; U.N., *Report of the Independent Inquiry*, 28.
[114] ICISS, *Research, Bibliography, Background*, 100.
[115] Ibid.
[116] U.N., *Report of the Independent Inquiry*, 30.
[117] Ibid.

respond to the genocide."[118] These are, however, not a comprehensive list of the failures identified by the Independent Inquiry.

With regard to Srebrenica, the execution of between 7 000 – 8 000 Bosnian Muslims in the space of one week in July 1995 by "Bosnian Serb and other forces,"[119] marks what is referred to as the "worst massacre that occurred in Europe since the months after World War II."[120] This case is significant for our purposes here, as at the time of the massacre, Srebrenica had been declared a 'safe area' by the U.N. in terms of Resolution 819 (1993) which was adopted on 16 April 1993.[121] On the need for action there was general agreement however, on the question of what form of action would be appropriate, agreement remained elusive.[122] The Secretary-General also understood that consensus within the Council was only possible with regards to "three broad areas, namely, the need to alleviate the consequences of war; the need to contain the conflict; and the need to promote the prospects for a negotiated peace settlement."[123]

During this process of searching for compromise within the Council, the establishment of "security zones, safe havens and protected areas for the Bosnian population,"[124] emerged as one of a number of proposals. On 16 April 1993, "the council adopted a draft resolution tabled by the non-aligned members as resolution 819 (1993) in which it demanded that"[125] Srebrenica and its surrounding area be treated by all factions and others as a safe area, and that the area "should be free from any armed attack or any other hostile act."[126] The resolution further called on "Bosnian Serb paramilitary units" to immediately cease armed attacks against Srebrenica, as well as "their immediate withdrawal from the areas surrounding Srebrenica." It also demanded that "the Federal Republic of Yugoslavia immediately cease the supply of military arms, equipment and services to the Bosnian Serb paramilitary units in the Republic of Bosnia and Herzegovina."[127]

---

[118] Ibid, 35.
[119] International Criminal Tribunal for the former Yugoslavia, "Facts About Srebrenica," accessed October 9, 2010, http://www.icty.org/x/file/Outreach/view_from_hague/jit_srebrenica_en.pdf
[120] Ibid.
[121] Report of the Secretary-General Pursuant to General Assembly Resolution 53/35, *The Fall of Srebrenica*, 18, U.N. Doc. A/54/549 (November 15, 1999).
[122] Ibid, 16.
[123] Ibid, 16.
[124] Ibid, 16.
[125] Ibid, 18.
[126] Ibid, 18.
[127] Ibid, 18.

Apart from Resolution 819 (1993), the UN Protection Force for the former Yugoslavia (UNPROFOR) concluded a demilitarization agreement between the Bosniacs and the Serbs whereby the Bosniac forces would surrender their arms to "UNPROFOR in return for the promise of a ceasefire, the insertion of a UNPROFOR company into Srebrenica, the evacuation of the seriously wounded and the seriously ill, unimpeded access for UNHCR and ICRC."[128] This agreement stipulated the terms whereby the demilitarization of Srebrenica would be carried out. However, it did not demarcate the area that was to be demilitarized.[129] The agreement was initiated by UNPROFOR because it was confronted by the situation on the ground whereby "the Serbs were in a position of complete military dominance around Srebrenica, and that the town and its population were at risk."[130] Two other resolutions adopted by the Council are significant, namely Resolution 824 (1993) and Resolution 836 (1993), but due to space constraints, these will not be discussed here. Under Resolution 836 (1993) "UNPROFOR was given an ambitious but ambiguous mandate to protect"[131] the safe areas which included Srebrenica, Sarajevo, Žepa, Tuzla, Bihać and Goražde (the latter four were declared safe areas under Resolution 824 (1993)), and furthermore, with regard to Resolution 819 (1993), the Council provided UNPROFOR with neither the resources nor the mandate to impose the demands of the resolution on the parties.[132]

Despite the adoption of Resolution 836 (1993) Bosnian Serbs continued attacks on safe areas until August 1995, and furthermore, the Serbs "continued to obstruct freedom of movement to all of the safe areas,"[133] for humanitarian convoys as well as UNPROFOR, "imposing a system of clearances, the principal effect of which was to limit the effectiveness of UNPROFOR and to slow down the delivery of humanitarian aid."[134] However, when provided with a presentation by the Secretariat, whereby it asserted that roughly 32 000 additional soldiers would be needed for the implementation of the safe area concept, the sponsors of Resolution 836 (1993), namely the US, the UK, Spain, the Russian Federation and France, opposed this view.[135] Thus UNPROFOR would get no additional troops from the sponsor states.[136] The fall of Srebrenica, from 6 – 11 July 1995, the killing of hundreds of unarmed Bosniac men and boys, which began on the 13th of July, and the mass executions

---

[128] Ibid, 19.
[129] Ibid, 19.
[130] Ibid, 19.
[131] ICISS, *Research, Bibliography, Background*, 92.
[132] U.N., *The Fall of Srebrenica*, 18.
[133] Ibid, 25.
[134] Ibid, 25.
[135] Ibid, 25.
[136] Ibid, 25.

which commenced on the 14th of July,[137] all point to the massive failings of the U.N. in its task to protect civilians in Srebrenica. The unwillingness by members of the Security Council as well as the sponsors of Resolution 836 (1993) to contribute the troop numbers for the adequate implementation of the safe area concept, as well the unwillingness to utilize force as a means to deter attacks on safe areas by Bosnian Serbs is by and large one reason why the Serbs were able to overrun Srebrenica with relative ease. The international community's response to the situation in Bosnia and Herzegovina by means of an arms embargo, humanitarian aid and the deployment of a peacekeeping force were entirely insufficient.[138]

Thus far the discussion in this section has focused on two prominent failures of the U.N. in terms of humanitarian intervention to stop or avert large-scale killing. In his millennium report, then Secretary-General of the U.N., Kofi Annan, referred to the cases of Rwanda and Srebrenica when addressing the dilemma of intervention.[139] The former Secretary-General laid down the challenge whereby he asks what the international community's response should by in such instances of severe human rights violations if humanitarian intervention does did in fact constitute "an unacceptable assault on sovereignty."[140] Annan recognized that both the defense of human rights and of sovereignty are principles which must enjoy support; however, in instances where these two principles are in conflict, this does not make clear which principle should enjoy primacy.[141] Although noting the contentious nature of humanitarian intervention, Annan asserted that "no legal principle – not even sovereignty – can ever shield crimes against humanity,"[142] and where peaceful attempts to put an end to such crimes "have been exhausted, the Security Council has a moral duty to act on behalf of the international community."[143]

It was this challenge to which the Canadian government, acting on the initiative and ingenuity of Foreign Minister Lloyd Axworthy, and together with "a group of major foundations"[144] established the ICISS,[145] which was tasked "to wrestle with the whole range of questions – legal, moral, operational and political – rolled up in this debate, to consult with the widest possible range of opinion around the world, and to bring back a report that would help

---

[137] Ibid, 57, 77, 80.
[138] Ibid, 105.
[139] Annan, 48.
[140] Ibid.
[141] Ibid.
[142] Ibid.
[143] Ibid.
[144] ICISS, *Responsibility to Protect*, VII.
[145] ICISS, *Responsibility to Protect*, VII; Evans, *The Responsibility to Protect*, 38; Bellamy, *Responsibility to Protect*, 36.

the Secretary-General and everyone else find some new common ground."[146] The ICISS would be responsible for formulating and outlining "appropriate and politically feasible international responses"[147] to severe human rights violations and to identify and set out mechanisms for the prevention of such violations.[148] Launched in September 2000, the Commission was given just one year to complete its work, and in December of 2001 the Commission published its report, 90 pages long, as well as a "400-page supplementary volume of research essays, bibliography, and background material, all under the title, *The Responsibility to Protect*."[149]

As has been mentioned, the Report has envisioned a re-conceptualisation of sovereignty, adding to it a fourth dimension, and expanding the concept to entail a threefold responsibility of states.[150] However, the genesis of the concept of sovereignty as responsibility does not lie with the ICISS, as its roots date back further to the early 1990s.[151] Francis Deng and Roberta Cohen are credited as the first to utilize the concept of responsibility to protect.[152] From 1992 – 2004, Deng served as the U.N. Secretary-General's Special Representative on Internally Displaced Persons (IDP), and then as the U.N. Secretary-General's Special Advisor on the Prevention of Genocide,[153] and Cohen, who later joined the Brookings Institute, faced the primary challenges of persuading host states to enhance the protection extended to IDPs and "how to work around the denial of assistance by sovereign authorities."[154] Recognising both sides of the problem, Deng asserted that firstly with regard to the humanitarian aspect, IDPs remain within the territorial boundaries of a state which is at war with itself, and those who do move to safer areas are treated as strangers, often harassed and discriminated against, and furthermore, individuals who have been uprooted from their homes "have been shown to be especially vulnerable to physical attack, sexual assault, abduction, disease and deprivation of basic life needs."[155] With regards to the somewhat problematic political status of IDPs,

---

[146] ICISS, *Responsibility to Protect*, VII.
[147] Bellamy, *Responsibility to Protect*, 36.
[148] Ibid.
[149] Evans, *The Responsibility to Protect*, 38.
[150] ICISS, Responsibility to Protect, 13; Grono, 623; Williams and Bellamy, 28.
[151] Evans, *The Responsibility to Protect*, 36; Alex J. Bellamy, "The Responsibility to Protect and the Problem of Military Intervention," *International Affairs* 84 (2008): 618; Nicholas J. Wheeler and Frazer Egerton, "The Responsibility to Protect: 'Precious Committment' or a Promise Unfilled?" *Global Responsibility to Protect* 1 (2009): 116.
[152] Evans, *The Responsibility to Protect*, 36; Wheeler and Egerton, 116; Alex J. Bellamy, "The Responsibility to Protect and the Problem of Military Intervention," *International Affairs* 84 (2008): 619; Bellamy, *Responsibility to Protect*, 21-2.
[153] Evans, *The Responsibility to Protect*, 36; Wheeler and Egerton, 116; Bellamy, *The Problem of Military Intervention*, 618; Bellamy, *Responsibility to Protect*, 21.
[154] Bellamy, *The Problem of Military Intervention*, 619.
[155] Francis M. Deng, "The Impact of State Failure on Migration," *Mediterranean Quarterly* 15(2004): 18.

Deng noted that not only is internal displacement caused by their own government, but IDPs are often beyond the international community's reach due to the "negative approach to sovereignty as a barrier against international involvement."[156] Although international human rights and humanitarian instruments "offer legally binding bases"[157] for assistance and international protection to needy populations within the territorial borders of their home state, these populations are by and large at the mercy of their state authorities for their general welfare and security.[158]

As a means to circumvent the use of sovereignty as a mechanism to obstruct the provision of international assistance for the internally displaced, Deng and Cohen developed the concept of 'sovereignty as responsibility.'[159] The starting point for this novel understanding of the relationship between fundamental human rights and sovereignty is the acknowledgement that the host state is allocated the primary responsibility for the protection and assistance of IDPs.[160] Deng and Cohen argued that no legitimate government could find fault with the assertion that it is charged with the responsibility of ensuring the wellbeing and security of its citizens – and in fact, no state argued against this claim.[161] In situations where a state is unable to discharge this responsibility, the two went further to argue that it should not only invite, but also welcome, international assistance, as this assistance in actual fact facilitates the "realisation of effective national sovereignty"[162] by enhancing the capacity of the state in terms of its ability to "fulfil its sovereign responsibilities,"[163] and furthermore allows the state in question to take up its place "as a legitimate member of international society."[164] In major crisis situations troubled or vulnerable states are faced with a choice: they can either cooperate with international organisations in an attempt to fulfil their sovereign responsibilities; or they can hamper and impede these efforts, thus sacrificing "their good standing and sovereign legitimacy."[165]

With regards to a particular threshold beyond which a state could be judged to have suffered a crisis of sovereignty, as well as what body was vested with the authority to make such a judgement, Deng and a number of his colleagues were less than clear. They did, however, maintain that the concept of "sovereignty as responsibility implied the existence of a

---

[156] Ibid, 20.
[157] Ibid, 20.
[158] Ibid, 20.
[159] Bellamy, *The Problem of Military Intervention*, 619; Bellamy, *Responsibility to Protect*, 22.
[160] Bellamy, *The Problem of Military Intervention*, 619; Bellamy, *Responsibility to Protect*, 22.
[161] Bellamy, *The Problem of Military Intervention*, 619; Bellamy, *Responsibility to Protect*, 22.
[162] Bellamy, *Responsibility to Protect*, 22.
[163] Ibid.
[164] Bellamy, *The Problem of Military Intervention*, 619.
[165] Ibid.

'higher authority capable of holding supposed sovereigns accountable,"[166] and furthermore, this authority is to prioritise the common good above its members' national interests.[167] Clearly, the U.N. Security Council is the body which fits this description best. The formulation of sovereignty as responsibility – and not simply in the traditional conceptualisation of the term which is preoccupied with territorial control – has resonated well with all the post-World War II "institutional developments associated with the establishment of the United Nations, membership of the U.N.,"[168] and specifically, "accession to its human rights instruments, which necessarily entails the voluntary acceptance of sovereignty-limiting obligations or responsibilities, both internally and externally."[169] This formulation of Deng and his collaborators – despite not receiving the "wider attention that was focused on *droit d'ingérence* or human security, or the ideas of Tony Blair or Kofi Annan," nevertheless became more of a "central conceptual underpinning"[170] of the R2P norm in its final conceptualisation, than any of the abovementioned contributions which emerged in the 1990s.

Sovereignty, according to the traditional Westphalian conceptualisation thereof, emphasises territorial rule, and locates "supreme legal and political authority with territorially delimited states."[171] Sovereignty, thus understood, entails the "rightful entitlement to exclusive, unqualified and supreme rule within a delimited territory."[172] It is exclusive to the extent that no ruler or state "had the right to intervene in the sovereign affairs of other nations;"[173] unqualified in so far as that within the territorial boundaries of their states, rulers enjoyed unqualified authority over their citizens; and finally, it is supreme in the sense that there exists no political or legal authority above the state.[174] The ICISS has, as has been mentioned before, proposed a re-conceptualisation of sovereignty, and borrowing Deng and Cohen's terminology, added a fourth dimension to it and envisioned a threefold responsibility of states.[175] This re-conceptualisation does not amount to a dilution or transfer of state sovereignty, but rather a necessary re-characterization "from *sovereignty as control* to *sovereignty as responsibility* in both internal functions and external duties."[176]

---

[166] Ibid, 620.
[167] Ibid, 620.
[168] Evans, *The Responsibility to Protect*, 37.
[169] Ibid.
[170] Ibid.
[171] Anthony McGrew, "Globalization and Global Politics," in *The Globalization of World Politics: An Introduction to International Relations*, 3rd ed., edited by John Baylis and Steve Smith (Oxford: Oxford University Press, 2005), 30.
[172] Ibid.
[173] Ibid.
[174] Ibid.
[175] ICISS, *The Responsibility to Protect*, 13; Grono, 623; Williams and Bellamy, 28.
[176] ICISS, *The Responsibility to Protect*, 13.

With regards to the threefold responsibility of states, the Report asserts that in the first instance this implies that states are charged with the responsibility of protecting and ensuring the lives and safety of its citizens, as well as with promoting their welfare.[177] Secondly, it suggests that national governments are not only responsible to their citizens internally, but are also externally responsible to the international community via the U.N.,[178] and finally, it means that states carry responsibility for their actions; in other words, "they are accountable for their acts of commission and omission."[179] The central proposition of the Report is that:

> State sovereignty implies responsibility, and the primary responsibility for the protection of its people lies with the state itself. Where a population is suffering serious harm, as a result of internal war, insurgency, repression or state failure, and the state in question is unwilling or unable to halt or avert it, the principle of non-intervention yields to the international responsibility to protect.[180]

With regards to the last part of final sentence, the Report asserts that in instances where a particular state is either unwilling or unable to discharge this responsibility, the state in question suffers an abrogation of sovereignty, and the responsibility to protect is transferred to the international community of states.[181]

By emphasising this novel re-characterization of sovereignty, the report has shifted the language of the debate around humanitarian intervention, and has replaced the concept of a "'right to intervene' with a responsibility to protect'."[182] Effecting a change in the "terminology from 'intervention' to 'protection',"[183] allows one to break with "the language of 'humanitarian intervention',"[184] an important step as the term has always been as significant cause for concern for humanitarian organisations, which have displayed deep resentment toward the association of military activity with 'humanitarian'.[185] Furthermore, changing the language of the debate and speaking of a 'responsibility to protect' instead of the 'right to intervene' presents at least four other significant advantages. Firstly, it implies an evaluation of the issues from the perspective of those in need of support,[186] and focuses attention on "the urgent needs of the potential beneficiaries of the action,"[187] instead of concentrating on the rights, claims

---

[177] Ibid.
[178] Ibid.
[179] Ibid.
[180] Ibid, XI.
[181] Badescu and Bergholm, 288; Lee Feinstein and Anne-Marie Slaughter, "A Duty to Prevent," *Foreign Affairs* 83 (2004): 141.
[182] Jeremy L. Levitt, "The Responsibility to Protect: A Beaver Without a Dam?" *Michigan Journal of International Law* 25 (2003): 157
[183] Gareth Evans and Mohamed Sahnoun, "The Responsibility to Protect," *Foreign Affairs* 81 (2002):101.
[184] Ibid.
[185] Ibid.
[186] Evans and Sahnoun, 101; Gelijn Molier, "Humanitarian Intervention and the Responsibility to Protect After 9/11," *Netherlands International Law Review* LIII (2006): 48.
[187] ICISS, *The Responsibility to Protect*, 16.

and prerogatives of the states considering intervention.[188] Secondly, framing it in the language of responsibility to protect implies that the primary responsibility lies with the state in question, and only where that state is either unwilling or unable to discharge this responsibility, or is the perpetrator itself, should the responsibility to act be taken up by the international community.[189] Thirdly, use of the 'responsibility to protect' language allows one to depart from an overly narrow focus on the act of intervention.[190] As an umbrella concept, the 'responsibility to protect' not only entails not only a 'responsibility to react', but also "the 'responsibility to prevent' and the 'responsibility to rebuild'."[191] The latter two dimensions have been substantially overlooked in the traditional debate on humanitarian intervention, and re-casting the spotlight on them "should help make the concept of reaction itself more palatable."[192] Finally, the language of the 'right to intervene' effectively functions to "trump sovereignty with intervention at the outset of the debate:" it displays a tendency to delegitimize and characterise dissent as anti-humanitarian and thereby stacks the odds in favour of intervention prior to the start of any debate or argument on the matter.[193]

In its redefinition of sovereignty, the ICISS has constructed the notion to serve "as a linking concept that bridges the divide between"[194] intervention by the international community and sovereignty.[195] The Reports asserts that the language of the 'right to intervene' is inherently more confrontational, and the above point relates to the Report's assertion regarding instances in which a state is either unwilling or unable to discharge its responsibility to protect, which then becomes the responsibility of the international community. This is the point which underlies Macfarlane et al.'s statement that the Report argues that the relationship between intervention for the purpose of protecting human rights and sovereignty is complementary instead of contradictory, as was suggested in much of the previous debate.[196] A final point regarding the ICISS and sovereignty is worth mentioning. Deng proposed in 1995 that state sovereignty has proceeded through four stages/phases since its origin in the Peace of Westphalia in 1648, where the concept of the modern state was initially formalized.[197] The first phase was characterised by "an absoluteness that extended both internally and externally

---

[188] Evans and Sahnoun, 101; ICISS, *The Responsibility to Protect*, 16; Molier, 48.
[189] Evans and Sahnoun, 101.
[190] Evans and Sahnoun, 101; ICISS, *The Responsibility to Protect*, 16; Molier, 48; Ramesh Thakur, "Iraq and the Responsibility to Protect," *Behind the Headlines* 62 (2004): 7.
[191] Evans and Sahnoun, 101.
[192] Ibid.
[193] ICISS, *The Responsibility to Protect*, 16.
[194] Ibid, 17.
[195] ICISS, *The Responsibility to Protect*, 17; David Chandler, "The Responsibility to Protect? Imposing the 'Liberal Peace'," *International Peacekeeping* 11 (2004): 65.
[196] Macfarlane, Thielking and Weiss, 978; Quinn, 34.
[197] Quinn, 14.

in the new international community."[198] The second stage, engendered by the establishment of democratic institutions and values that necessitated "international accountability for human rights,"[199] and as a result prompted a "reduction of the absolute sovereignty"[200] which characterised the first stage. The third stage is characterised by a return to an emphasis on state sovereignty and a re-assertion thereof by states' whose behaviour and actions in the domestic realm could warrant international criticism.[201] Deng's final stage is the contemporary one, in which the international community acknowledges that a "state's sovereignty must be reconciled with the state's responsibility for the protection of its citizens' human rights."[202] Quinn postulates that the Report has attempted to "pull the world toward a fifth stage where state sovereignty routinely acquiesces to the international responsibility to protect."[203] Thus one sees that not only has the ICISS sought to redefine sovereignty, but in the process it has created a fifth stage of sovereignty in which, as the Report argues, "where a population is suffering serious harm...and the state in question is unwilling or unable to halt or avert it, the principle of non-intervention yields to the international responsibility to protect."[204]

Early in the Report the ICISS sets out the core principles which underpin the R2P, and among these the Commission identifies the basic principles of R2P, the foundations on which the principle is built, the elements/components which make up R2P, and finally its priorities. Starting with the basic principles, although these were identified earlier in the preceding section, I believe the discussion here warrants another mention: (i) "State sovereignty implies responsibility, and the primary responsibility for the protection of its people lies with the state itself,"[205] and (ii) "Where a population is suffering serious harm, as a result of internal war, insurgency, repression or state failure, and the state in question is unwilling or unable to halt or avert it, the principle of non-intervention yields to the international responsibility to protect."[206] The first of these principles builds, as has been mentioned, on the work of Francis Deng and his colleagues, and although the concept did not originate in the workings of the ICISS, the Report has succeeded in placing "the concept squarely in the debate over the efficacy of humanitarian intervention."[207] The significance of this principle is by and large discussed in the preceding section, and this relates to the Report's argument for a re-

---

[198] Ibid.
[199] Ibid.
[200] Ibid.
[201] Ibid.
[202] Ibid.
[203] Ibid.
[204] ICISS, *The Responsibility to Protect*, XI.
[205] Ibid.
[206] Ibid.
[207] Levitt, 159.

characterization of sovereignty as well as the change that it has brought about in the language of the sovereignty – intervention debate. The second basic principle is definitive and bold – the report argues that the non-intervention principle (a *jus cogens* norm) acquiesces to the "international responsibility to protect,"[208] which is at best a "customary international law norm...(as opposed to the pre-emptory nature of a *jus cogens* norm)."[209] This is a daring step as it raises such responsibility to a level where it is perceived as a 'duty' and "anoints it with a status that transcends the more well-established 'right to intervention' or humanitarian intervention."[210]

The foundation of R2P rests on four main pillars: (i) "obligations inherent in the concept of sovereignty;"[211] (ii) the responsibility of the Security Council, under Article 24 of the UN Charter, for the maintenance of international peace and security;"[212] (iii) specific legal obligations under human rights and human protection declarations, covenants and treaties, international humanitarian law and national law;"[213] and (iv) the developing practice of states, regional organizations and the Security Council itself."[214] Although one would be hard pressed to find a state that would argue with the first three pillars, the fourth is more contentious and as a result warrants further analysis. Depending on how regional organisation's developing practices are weighted and interpreted, as well as the Security Council's responses to these practices, the argument can already be made that R2P has acquired normative status.[215] Unilateral intervention (lacking prior Security Council authorization) by regional organisations and states in Africa, specifically the Economic Community of West African States (ECOWAS) "and its Cease-Fire Monitoring Group (ECOMOG),"[216] coupled with the African Union (AU)'s interventionist law, supports the idea of the "existence of the doctrine of humanitarian intervention."[217] By its very nature, a norm of intervention is in conflict with the traditional non-intervention norm as articulated in the U.N. Charter, yet it is nevertheless 'legally oxidised' by the Security Council's "consistent practice of retroactively authorizing otherwise illegal (under UN law) African interventions."[218] In fact, it is Security Council practice that is eroding, first, "the mantle of state sovereignty"[219] by endorsing humanitarian

---

[208] ICISS, *The Responsibility to Protect*, XI.
[209] Levitt, 159.
[210] Ibid.
[211] ICISS, *The Responsibility to Protect*, XI.
[212] Ibid.
[213] Ibid.
[214] Ibid.
[215] Levitt, 160.
[216] Ibid.
[217] Ibid.
[218] Ibid.
[219] Ibid.

interventions, even those carried out beyond the ambit of its authority, and second, "the UN Charter principle of non-intervention, by ex post facto authorizing such interventions."[220]

Turning to the elements/components of R2P, the Report embraces three key and specific responsibilities: (i) "the responsibility to prevent: to address both the root causes and direct causes of internal conflict and other man-made crises putting populations at risk,"[221] (ii) "the responsibility to react: to respond to situations of compelling human need with appropriate measures, which may include coercive measures like sanctions and international prosecution and in extreme cases military intervention,"[222] and (iii) "the responsibility to rebuild: to provide, particularly after a military intervention, full assistance with recovery, reconstruction and reconciliation, addressing the causes of the harm the intervention was designed to halt or avert."[223] Although these are not novel responsibilities, apart from the language that is, they correspond to the "better known concepts of conflict prevention, management, and resolution."[224] The two priorities which the Report identifies are related to the responsibilities which it embraces, and are as follows: (i) "Prevention is the single most important dimension of the responsibility to protect: prevention options should always be exhausted before intervention is contemplated, and more commitment and resources must be devoted to it,"[225] and (ii) "the exercise of the responsibility to both prevent and react should always involve less intrusive and coercive measures being considered before more coercive and intrusive ones are applied."[226] This is somewhat puzzling given that the Report's aim to identify new means of responding to "pre-existing humanitarian crises"[227] and the protection of vulnerable populations. Such an overbearing focus on prevention requires that powerful states invest in "early warning systems, preventative deployment missions, and other forms of institution building"[228] in unstable and volatile states and conflict zones where they have no significant national interest, which may inevitably result in the problem of a lack of political will.

The Report asserts that in certain cases the responsibility to react may involve a resort to coercive military measures, but questions what should be regarded as an exceptional or

---

[220] Ibid.
[221] ICISS, *The Responsibility to Protect*, XI.
[222] Ibid.
[223] Ibid.
[224] Levitt, 162.
[225] ICISS, *The Responsibility to Protect*, XI.
[226] Ibid.
[227] Levitt, 165.
[228] Ibid.

extreme case.[229] In providing a solution, the Report takes as its starting point the principle of non-intervention, and argues that exceptions to the non-intervention principle should be restricted and that "military intervention for human protection purposes must be regarded as an exceptional and extraordinary measure,"[230] and is to be warranted only in cases where "serious or irreparable harm [is] occurring to human beings, or imminently likely to occur."[231] With regards to the principles for military intervention, the Commission has identified six criteria that need to be met in order to justify military intervention, these are the just cause threshold, the precautionary principles, right authority and operational principles.

The Report contends that the just cause threshold for military intervention for the purposes of human protection is satisfied where a state or states aim to halt or avert: (i) "large-scale loss of life, actual or apprehended, with genocidal intent or not, which is the product of either deliberate state action, state neglect or inability to act, or a failed state situation; or"[232] (ii) "large-scale 'ethnic cleansing', actual or apprehended, whether carried out by killing, forced expulsion, acts of terror, or rape, or any combination thereof."[233] Evans and Sahnoun[234] have argued that there is both a practical political and a conceptual rational for setting the bar for just cause so high. Conceptually, they assert that "military intervention must be very exceptional,"[235] and with regards to the other line of reasoning, Evans and Sahnoun contend that if intervention is to occur when it is most needed, "it cannot be called on too often."[236] The Report fails to quantify in either socio-political or legal terms what 'large-scale loss of life' refers to,[237] which leads one to ask: if, as the Report states, "prevention is the single most important dimension of the responsibility to protect," is it then not contradictory that a 'large-scale loss of life' act as a pre-requisite for saving lives?[238] Evans and Sahnoun have argued that although the Report does not stipulate what is meant by 'large-scale', but the Commission is nevertheless clear in its "belief that military action can be legitimate as an anticipatory measure in response to clear evidence of likely large-scale killing or ethnic cleansing."[239] Were it not for this possibility, these authors argue, the international community would find

---

[229] ICISS, *The Responsibility to Protect*, 31.
[230] Ibid, 32.
[231] Ibid, 32.
[232] Ibid, XII.
[233] Ibid, XII.
[234] Evans and Sahnoun, 103.
[235] Ibid.
[236] Ibid.
[237] Levitt, 166.
[238] Ibid.
[239] Evans and Sahnoun, 103.

itself in a morally untenable situation where it will be required to wait for the outbreak of genocide before being able to undertake action necessary to stop it.[240]

Turning to the precautionary principles, the Report identifies four, namely, right intention, last resort, proportional means and finally, reasonable prospects.[241] With regards to right intention, the Report states, "the primary purpose of the intervention, whatever other motives intervening states may have, must be to halt or avert human suffering. Right intention is better assured with multilateral operations, clearly supported by regional opinion and the victims concerned."[242] In terms of the second precautionary principle, last resort, the Report postulates that, "military intervention can only be justified when every non-military option for the prevention or peaceful resolution of the crisis has been explored, with reasonable grounds for believing lesser measures would not have succeeded."[243] Proportional means is the third precautionary principle which the Report identifies and frames it as, "the scale, duration and intensity of the planned military intervention should be the minimum necessary to secure the defined human protection objective."[244] The final precautionary principle is reasonable prospects, and with regards to it the Report asserts that "there must be reasonable chance of success in halting or averting the suffering which has justified the intervention, with the consequences of action not likely to be worse than the consequences of inaction."[245] These precautionary principles are based in 'just war' doctrine and are by and large incontestable, and serves as a "basic but sound framework to assess the legal and political efficacy of intervention."[246]

Despite the 'just war' doctrine forming the foundation for these principles, they nevertheless appear to embrace peacekeeping doctrine that has materialised from state practice since the Cold War's end, and in this context the first two elements enjoy the most relevance.[247] The acknowledgement in the 'right intention' principle that it is often the case that intervening states are driven by mixed motives to do so, and that local and regional opinion is pivotal to "the success of any enforcement operations, is refreshing."[248] The reasonable prospects

---

[240] Ibid, 103-4.
[241] ICISS, *The Responsibility to Protect*, XII.
[242] Ibid.
[243] Ibid.
[244] Ibid.
[245] Ibid.
[246] Levitt, 168.
[247] Ibid, 169.
[248] Ibid, 169.

principle is unique in the sense that it recasts focus on the significance of states to thoroughly assess the situation in conflict zones or target states prior to undertaking intervention.[249]

The question of right authority is to a considerable degree the most crucial of the issues that make up the debate on humanitarian intervention,[250] and it is without question the most controversial and difficult principle to apply.[251] As articulated in the Report, the right authority principles are as follows:

> A. There is no better or more appropriate body than the United Nations Security Council to authorize military intervention for human protection purposes. The task is not to find alternatives to the Security Council as a source of authority, but to make the Security Council work better than it has.
> B. Security Council authorization should in all cases be sought prior to any military intervention action being carried out. Those calling for an intervention should formally request such authorization, or have the Council raise the matter on its own initiative, or have the Secretary-General raise it under Article 99 of the UN Charter.
> C. The Security Council should deal promptly with any request for authority to intervene where there are allegations of large scale loss of human life or ethnic cleansing. It should in this context seek adequate verification of facts or conditions on the ground that might support military intervention.
> D. The Permanent Five members of the Security Council should agree not to apply their veto power, in matters where their vital interests are not involved, to obstruct the passage of resolutions authorising military intervention for human protection purposes for which there is otherwise majority support.
> E. If the Security Council rejects a proposal or fails to deal with it in reasonable time, alternative options are:
> - I. Consideration of the matter by the General Assembly in Emergency Special Session under the "Uniting for Peace" procedure; and
> - II. Action within an area of jurisdiction by regional or sub-regional organizations under Chapter VIII of the Charter,

---

[249] Ibid, 169.
[250] Ibid, 169.
[251] Evans and Sahnoun, 106.

subject to their seeking subsequent authorization from the Security Council.

F. The Security Council should take into account all its deliberations, that if it fails to discharge its responsibility to protect in conscience-shocking situations crying out for action, concerned states may not rule out other means to meet the gravity and urgency of the situation – and that the stature and credibility of the United Nations may suffer thereby.[252]

Given the Security Council's history of failing to act and literally allowing a number of states to collapse and millions of people to die – the cases of Rwanda and Srebrenica which are discussed above provide examples of this – makes the ICISS's determination that no 'more appropriate' body other than the Security Council exists "to authorize military interventions and that prior authorization 'should be sought in all cases'" somewhat hard to accept.[253]

Lastly, with regards to the operational principles that the Report has put forward, these are as follows:

A. Clear objectives; clear unambiguous mandate at all times; and resources to match.
B. Common military approach among involved partners; unity of command; clear and unequivocal communications and chain of command.
C. Acceptance of limitations; incrementalism and gradualism in the application of force, the objective being protection of a population, not defeat of a state.
D. Rules of engagement which fit the operational concept; are precise; reflect the principle of proportionality; and involve total adherence to international humanitarian law.
E. Acceptance that force protection cannot become the principle objective.
F. Maximum possible coordination with humanitarian organizations.[254]

Few scholars, policy makers or military officials would find fault with such a comprehensive list, as the idea of a more holistic and novel operations doctrine grounded in the responsibility

---

[252] ICISS, *The Responsibility to Protect*, XII-XIII.
[253] Levitt, 170.
[254] ICISS, The Responsibility to Protect, XIII.

to protect has been perceived as a welcome development.[255] The just cause thresholds and the precautionary principles were intended to serve three principal functions, the first being that in an effort to avoid future situations such as that of Rwanda, the just cause thresholds were designed to "create expectations about the circumstances in which the international community – primarily the UN Security Council – should become engaged in major humanitarian catastrophes, consider intervening with force and constrain permanent members from casting pernicious vetoes for selfish reasons."[256] Secondly, in response to the need to prevent future situations such as that of Kosovo, where the U.N. Security Council was paralysed by veto, "the criteria provided a pathway for legitimizing intervention not authorized by the Security Council."[257] Finally, one of the foremost commissioners of the ICISS, Ramesh Thakur, asserted that the criteria should be perceived as restricting the ability of governments to "'abuse' R2P and limiting the scope of potential Security Council interventionalism."[258] Thakur believes that the criteria would serve the dual functions of firstly making "it more difficult for coalitions of the willing to appropriate the language of humanitarianism for geopolitical and unilateral interventions,"[259] and secondly, making the "Security Council deliberations more transparent."[260]

The primary focus of this chapter has been the ICISS and R2P, and began with a discussion of the origins of the concept of sovereignty as responsibility, providing a background to the terminology which the ICISS borrowed and built on. From there focus shifted to sovereignty as responsibility as the ICISS developed and utilised the term. In this section, the Report's central normative tenet, namely that states have a responsibility to protect their citizens, and where a state is either unwilling or unable to discharge this responsibility, the responsibility to protect then falls on the wider international community,[261] was discussed. The shift in the language of the debate around humanitarian intervention which the ICISS has engendered has been briefly focused on, as well as four key advantages that this presents. The final two sections of this chapter have focused on the basic principles of R2P and its principles for military intervention. Although some form of discussion and analysis has accompanied some but not all of the principles discussed in the last two sections of this chapter, space

---

[255] Levit, 174.
[256] Bellamy, *The Problem of Military Intervention*, 625.
[257] Ibid.
[258] Ibid.
[259] Ramesh Thakur, "A Shared Responsibility for a More Secure World," *Global Governance* II (2005): 284, quoted in Alex J. Bellamy, "The Responsibility to Protect and the Problem of Military Intervention," *International Affairs* 84 (2008): 625.
[260] Bellamy, *The Problem of Military Intervention*, 625.
[261] ICISS, *The Responsibility to Protect*, XI.

constraints has limited to the ability to provide fuller and more thorough discussion and analysis of these.

Chapter 4

As has been mentioned, R2P has progressed from inception in 2001 to widespread international acceptance in 2005 at the World Summit, remarkably quickly,[262] but also, that as endorsed at the 2005 World Summit, R2P is significantly different from its articulation in the ICISS report. This chapter aims to provide a discussion of the most significant events and arguments that have informed the debate around R2P and which have influenced the formulation of R2P in the World Summit Outcome Document. To this end, the chapter starts with a discussion of R2P as endorsed at the 2005 World Summit and articulated in its outcome document. From there the discussion shifts to the war on terror and the 2003 war in Iraq, with focus being placed on the effects these events have had on global buy-in of R2P, and the third section deals with the crisis in Darfur. The final section, although brief, deals with the issue of Security Council buy-in.

The central theme of the ICISS report has been mentioned above, and will not be repeated here; however, the notion was introduced in the context of a debate on U.N. reform in December 2004.[263] Referring to the international responses to successive humanitarian crises from that in Somalia to Darfur, Sudan, in its report entitled, *A More Secure World: Our Shared Responsibility*, HLP stated that:

> There is a growing acceptance that while sovereign governments have the primary responsibility to protect their own citizens from such catastrophes, when they are unable or unwilling to do so that responsibility should be taken up by the wider international community – with it spanning a continuum involving prevention, response to violence, if necessary, and rebuilding shattered societies.[264]

The HLP endorsed the emerging norm acknowledging a shared international responsibility to protect, which embraces not only "the 'right to intervene' of any State, but the 'responsibility to protect' of *every* State when it comes to people suffering from avoidable catastrophe."[265] The U.N. Secretary-General endorsed this finding in his report, *In Larger Freedom: Towards Development, Security and Human rights for All*, which advanced the notion that the security of humanity and that of states are indivisible and that collective action was the only solution to

---

[262] Bannon, 1158-9; Grono, 622; Mamdani, 55.
[263] Carsten Stahn, "Responsibility to Protect: Political Rhetoric or emerging Legal Norm," *The American Journal of International Law* 101 (2007): 99.
[264] A More Secure World: Our Shared Responsibility, Report of the High-Level Panel on Threats, Challenges and Change, 65-66, U.N. Doc. A/59/565 (2004), accessed June 26, 2010, http://www.un.org/secureworld/report/pdf.
[265] Ibid, 65.

the threats that humanity faces.[266] This embrace of the doctrine of R2P by the HLP, the Secretary-General, as well as by the AU and the European Union (EU) effectively set the stage for and culminated in the endorsement of R2P by the United Nations General Assembly at the World Summit in 2005,[267] in paragraphs 138 and 139 of its outcome document, formulated as:

> 138. Each individual State has the responsibility to protect its populations from genocide, war crimes, ethnic cleansing and crimes against humanity. This responsibility entails the prevention of such crimes, including their incitement, through appropriate and necessary means. We accept that responsibility and act in accordance with it. The international community should, as appropriate, encourage and help states to exercise this responsibility and support the United Nations in establishing an early warning capacity.
>
> 139. The international community, through the United Nations, also has the responsibility to use appropriate diplomatic, humanitarian and other peaceful means, in accordance with Chapters VI and VIII of the Charter, to help protect populations from genocide, war crimes, ethnic cleansing, and crimes against humanity. In this context, we are prepared to take collective action, in a timely and decisive manner, through the Security Council, in accordance with the Charter, including Chapter VII, on a case-by-case basis and in cooperation with relevant regional organizations as appropriate, should peaceful means be inadequate and national authorities manifestly fail to protect their populations from genocide, war crimes, ethnic cleansing, and crimes against humanity. We stress the need for the General Assembly to continue consideration of the responsibility to protect populations from genocide, war crimes, ethnic cleansing and crimes against humanity and its implications, bearing in mind the principles of the Charter and international law. We also intend to commit ourselves, as necessary and appropriate, to helping States build capacity to protect their populations from genocide, war crimes, ethnic cleansing and crimes against humanity and to assisting those which are under stress before crises and conflicts break out.[268]

In the above two paragraphs, the 2005 World Summit Outcome Document has set out the three fundamental pillars of the R2P concept, namely, (i) "the responsibility of each individual state to protect its population from genocide, war crimes, ethnic cleansing, and crimes against humanity and their incitement;"[269] (ii) "the responsibility of the international community to undertake peaceful collective action to help states to exercise this responsibility, including concerted long-term capacity-building efforts and short-term preventive diplomacy;"[270] and (iii) "the responsibility of the international community to be prepared to take collective action in a timely and decisive manner through the UN Security Council, in accordance with the UN Charter, if national authorities are manifestly failing to protect their populations from these four crimes."[271]

---

[266] In Larger Freedon: Towards Development, Security and Human Rights for All, Report of the Secretary-General, paras. 16-22, U.N. Doc A/59/2005 (2005), accessed June 26, 2010, http://www.un.org/largerfreedom/contents.htm
[267] Grono, 623.
[268] U.N. General Assembly, paras. 138-9.
[269] Actualising the Responsibility to Protect, 43rd Conference on the United Nations of the Next Decade, (2008), 2, accessed June 26, 2010, http://ssm.com/abstract=1576639
[270] Ibid.
[271] Ibid.

Termed 'R2P-Lite' by Thomas Weiss,[272] Badescu and Bergholm assert that the 2005 endorsement of R2P is without question a watered-down version of that articulated in the Report.[273] With regards to the key differences between the concept as advanced in the Report, and the principle as endorsed by world leaders, Alex Bellamy states that:

> In the latter form, R2P no longer proposed criteria to guide decision-making about when to intervene; there is no code of conduct for the use of the veto; and there is no opening for coercive measures not authorized by the Security Council. The threshold on when R2P is transferred from the host state to the international society was raised from the point at which the host state proved itself 'unable and unwilling' to protect its own citizens to that at which the state was 'manifestly failing' in its responsibility to do so. Finally, the idea that R2P implies responsibilities – even obligations – on the part of the international society and especially the Security Council was all but removed, with the Council committed only to 'standing ready' to act when necessary.[274]

The manner in which the U.S. has pursued the war on terror and waged war in Iraq since 2003 has left many an observer uncomfortable – or rather, more uncomfortable – with the idea of a responsibility to protect.[275] The *ex post facto* justification on either humanitarian or R2P grounds for the invasion of Iraq in 2003 by the U.S., U.K. and Australia, as evidence for both weapons of mass destruction (WMD) and for ties between Saddam Hussein and Al Qaeda that failed to materialize, has been the single biggest obstacle to international buy-in on R2P, and largely undermined attempts to reach consensus on the matter.[276] The war against Iraq does not, however, meet the criteria for either humanitarian intervention or R2P.[277] The war on terror and that in Iraq have had "three stifling effects on that necessary normative conversation."[278] In the first instance, "the selective use of the Security Council has been compounded by Washington's and London's decision to go to war against Iraq"[279] without authorisation from the Security Council. Use of the Council in an *a la carte* fashion creates problems for those states seeking increased consistency with regards to the "application of international norms."[280] Iraq certainly is a conversation stopper for a large number of critics

---

[272] Thomas G. Weiss, Humanitarian Intervention (Cambridge: Polity Press, 2007), 117.
[273] Badescu and Bergholm, 291.
[274] Bellamy, *The Problem of Military Intervention*, 623.
[275] Evans, From Humanitarian Intervention, 717; Weiss, *R2P After 9/11*, 748.
[276] Macfarlane, Thielking and Weiss, 984; Maria Banda, *The Responsibility to Protect: Moving the Agenda Forward* (Ottawa: United Nations Association in Canada, 2007), 10; Gareth Evans, "When is it Right to Fight?" *Survival* 46 (2004): 70-71; Gareth Evans, "From Humanitarian Intervention to the Responsibility to Protect," Wisconsin International Law Journal 24 (2006): 717.
[277] Macfarlane, Thielking and Weiss, 984; Eric A. Heinze, "Humanitarian Intervention and the War in Iraq: Norms, Discourse and State Practice," Parameters (Spring 2006): 30; Kenneth Roth, "War in Iraq: Not a Humanitarian Intervention," 1-13, accessed June 28, 2010, http://www.unhcr.org/refworld/pdfid/402ba99f4.pdf; Kenneth Roth, "Was the Iraq War a Humanitarian Intervention?" Journal of Military Ethics 5 (2006): 84, 86, 88.
[278] Weiss, *R2P After 9/11*, 749.
[279] Ibid.
[280] Ibid.

when the discussion focuses on the possibility of introducing a measure of flexibility in the criteria for intervention or "setting aside the non-intervention principle."[281]

Secondly, slick rhetoric about the wars in Iraq and on terror implies an increased need for more sober analysis, for there is a very real threat of "contaminating the legitimate idea of humanitarian intervention by association,"[282] especially with the ex post facto and spurious humanitarian justifications for the invasion of Iraq which have emanated from Washington and London. As a result, it has become progressively harder since 2001 to oppose those who are hesitant with regards to codifying norms which relate to the use of "military force for human protection purposes."[283] The Bush doctrine has widely been regarded as such a dominant threat, emphasising pre-emptive and in some cases preventive self-defence, that it warrants a renewal of the non-intervention norm rather than a reduction in the mantle of sovereignty, despite a humanitarian rationale.[284] Unveiled in September 2002, the U.S. National Security Strategy limits any future discussion regarding the use of force for human protection purposes, as the Bush doctrine has effectively enhanced fears regarding U.S. dominance, as well as of the chaos that may well result "if what is sauce for the U.S. goose were to become sauce for many other would-be interventionist ganders."[285] One likely outcome of U.S. articulation of interventionist doctrines will be that states will become even more cautious than before "about accepting any doctrine, including on humanitarian intervention or on the responsibility to protect, that could be seen as opening the door to a general pattern of interventionism."[286]

Thirdly, and somewhat related, the likelihood of a shift in the General Assembly "toward a consensus resolution on criteria has also stalled."[287] The version of R2P that was endorsed at the World Summit omitted the criteria for the use of military force and insisted on the approval of the Security Council, and evidence points to Washington's "refusal to establish a doctrine that might function either as an automatic trigger or as a drag on the American use of force,"[288] meaning that the R2P just cause thresholds and precautionary principles could act to restrain "Washington's flexibility in determining when and where to intervene."[289]

---

[281] Ibid.
[282] Ibid, 749-50.
[283] Ibid, 750
[284] Macfarlane, Theilking and Weiss, 984; Weiss, *R2P After 9/11*, 750.
[285] Adam Roberts, "The United Nations and Humanitarian Intervention," *Humanitarian Intervention and International Relations* 90 (2004), quoted in Thomas G. Weiss, "R2P After 9/11 and the World Summit," *Wisconsin International Law Journal* 24 (2006): 750.
[286] Ibid.
[287] Weiss, *R2P After 9/11*, 750.
[288] Ibid.
[289] Ibid.

Ramesh Thakur has argued, as is mentioned in the preceding chapter, that consensus regarding criteria would limit state capacity to abuse R2P,[290] and "would make it more difficult for states to wrap themselves disingenuously in a humanitarian blanket for purely self interested interventions."[291] Thakur makes an intriguing suggestion, which is however, "beside the point because politics in the General Assembly have postponed the discussion *sine die*."[292] A final point regarding particularly the war in Iraq deserves mention. Taking Thakur's argument as a starting point, it is ironic that the humanitarian justification for the war in Iraq by the U.S. and U.K. has left many states, especially in the global South, suspicious of R2P and cautious of committing to the principle.[293] The point is that these states view the use of humanitarian justification for the war in Iraq as a Trojan horse to "mask neo-liberal ambitions,"[294] with the result that it has "almost choked at birth what many were hoping was an emerging norm justifying intervention on the basis of the principle of 'responsibility to protect'."[295]

The crisis in Darfur in which the Sudanese government along with its 'janjaweed' militia carried out what the U.N. has termed a 'reign of terror,' erupted in 2003.[296] This campaign has claimed over 250 000 lives and more than 2 million people have been displaced as a result of the conflict.[297] Although the Darfur case qualifies as an 'R2P situation'[298], and is regarded by some as the R2P's first test,[299] the crisis there has also impacted on the evolution of the R2P in two ways. Firstly, use of the language of R2P in the Darfur debates "has done little to forge consensus or overcome the struggle between sovereignty and human rights."[300] Secondly, and this is related to the impact of the humanitarian justification for the war in Iraq on international consensus on the R2P, it has diminished the moral standing and credibility of the U.S. and U.K., thereby undermining their standing as norm carriers.[301] With regards to the first, the language of R2P was employed by both opponents and advocates of intervention (in the Darfur case), and has allowed those opposed to intervention to "legitimate their actions by reference to the prevailing normative order."[302] It has enabled the traditional opponents to

---

[290] Bellamy, *The Problem of Military Intervention*, 625.
[291] Weiss, *R2P After 9/11*, 751.
[292] Ibid.
[293] Bellamy, *Trojan Horse*, 39; Williams and Bellamy, *Responsibility to Protect*, 36.
[294] Bellamy, *Trojan Horse*, 39; Williams and Bellamy, *Responsibility to Protect*, 36.
[295] Evans, *Right to Fight*, 63.
[296] Alex J. Bellamy and Nicholas J. Wheeler, "Humanitarian Intervention in World Politics," accessed June 28, 2010, http://www.cadair.aber.ac.uk/dspace/bitstream/2160/1925/1/Wheeler,%2520Bellamy.pdf
[297] Bellamy and Wheeler; Grono, 624.
[298] Evans, *The Responsibility to Protect*, 61.
[299] David Lanz, "Conflict Management and Opportunity Cost: The International Response to the Darfur Crisis," *FRIDE* (September 2008): 3.
[300] Bellamy, *Trojan Horse*, 33.
[301] Ibid, 32.
[302] Ibid, 52.

intervention to substitute the essentially "discredited 'sovereignty-as-absolute'-type arguments" [303] against intervention in extreme humanitarian crises with arguments relating to whom was primarily responsible for the protection of civilians in Darfur.[304] In the context of the debate over Darfur, this argument was employed to reject any outside involvement other than that approved by the Sudanese government.[305]

Returning to the Report, the ICISS states that the devolution of the responsibility to protect from the host government to the Security Council should be informed by what it describes as a "simple empirical test:"[306] when the host government is either unwilling or unable to protect its citizens.[307] In practice, this was intensely disputed, and although hardly any states reject publicly the notion that the "Security Council should act to halt genocide or mass murder,"[308] forging a consensus regarding when a threshold has been crossed has proven complex and complicated. As mentioned above, one of the key differences between the R2P concept as articulated in the Report and that endorsed at the 2005 World Summit is that the "threshold on when R2P is transferred from the host state to international society was raised from the point at which the host state proved itself 'unable and unwilling' to protect its own citizens to that at which the state was 'manifestly failing' in its responsibility to do so."[309] Thus the situation in Darfur along with arguments from the Sudanese government, the League of Arab States, the A.U. and, on occasion, U.N. officials, that primary responsibility to protect Darfur's civilians remains with the government of Sudan, has engendered a shift from the ICISS's apparently straightforward test to a wording thereof which is undoubtedly less clear, perhaps deliberately so in order to forestall the transfer of R2P to the international community and averting an encroachment on the sovereignty of the host state.

With regards to the second way in which the crisis in Darfur has influenced the evolution of the R2P, the debates around how to respond to this crisis provide evidence that the credibility of the U.K. and the U.S. as "humanitarian intervention norm carriers"[310] has diminished significantly as a result of the war in Iraq.[311] The point is that if the credibility of those states most closely "associated with the new norm is undermined by perceptions that they have abused it or raised it for primarily self-serving purposes, the process of normative

---

[303] Ibid, 52.
[304] Ibid.
[305] Ibid.
[306] Ibid.
[307] ICISS, The Responsibility to Protect, XI.
[308] Bellamy, *Trojan Horse*, 52.
[309] Bellamy, *The Problem of Military Intervention*, 623.
[310] Bellamy, *Trojan Horse*, 51.
[311] Bellamy, Trojan Horse, 37, 51; Scott Strauss, "Darfur and the Genocide Debate," *Foreign Affairs* 84 (2005): 128.

change is likely to be slowed or reversed."[312] What this means is that by diminishing their credibility as norm carriers, the war in Iraq has not only reduced the ability of the U.S. and the U.K. to secure international consensus on and commitment to the R2P, but also, as is the case with the effect of justifying that war in humanitarian terms, has left the international community, especially states in the global South, deeply suspicious of the principle.[313] What has compounded these perceptions has been the ability of the Sudanese government to portray "American activism on Darfur as analogous with its strategy in Iraq: both were oil-oriented and anti-Islamic."[314] While this may have served to strengthen Middle Eastern and African hostility to the notion of western intervention in Darfur, it has added to the weakening of the moral standing of those states associated with the invasion of Iraq in 2003.[315] As a result, a significant number of states in the developing world "lost their initial enthusiasm for R2P," with some suggesting "that it resembled a 'Trojan horse' for big power meddling,"[316] and others fearful that they themselves might become potential targets of future intervention.

This point speaks to the reason for my pursuing the issue of the evolution of the R2P in this thesis. As mentioned in the introduction, based on this point an argument can be made that the international system is currently experiencing a shift in the authors of the rules of the system. The end of World War II and the emergence of the U.S. as the global authority saw it play a central role in the establishment of the U.N. and the Bretton Woods institutions,[317] where it also played a leading role in underwriting the rules which govern these institutions – rules which govern the international system.[318] However, as is seen here, the moral standing and credibility of the U.S. and the U.K. – also a leading player in the international system – as norm carriers have weakened and diminished significantly. Furthermore, with regards to the crisis in Darfur, these states recognised "their diminished credibility as norm carriers," and realized that this would hamper and obstruct either state in its attempts to take a leading role in "building a council consensus on action."[319] This serves to add credence to the claim that the international system is undergoing a change in the authors of the rules of the system.

---

[312] Bellamy, *Trojan Horse*, 32-3.
[313] Banda, 10, 19-20.
[314] Bellamy, *Responsibility to Protect*, 69.
[315] Ibid, 69-70.
[316] Badescu and Bergholm, 294.
[317] Paul Taylor and Devon Curtis, "The United Nations," in *The Globalization of World Politics: An Introduction to International Relations*, 3rd ed., edited by John Baylis and Steve Smith (Oxford: Oxford University Press, 2005), 406; Ngaire Woods, "International Political Economy in an Age of Globalization," in *The Globalization of World Politics: An Introduction to International Relations*, 3rd ed., edited by John Baylis and Steve Smith (Oxford: Oxford University Press, 2005), 326.
[318] Taylor and Curtis, 406-7; Woods, 326-7.
[319] Bellamy, *Trojan Horse*, 51.

Focusing on the diminished credibility of these states as norm carriers with regard to commitment to and consensus on R2P, as well as their self-acknowledged lack of ability to build Security Council consensus regarding intervention in Darfur may seem to be placing too much emphasis on only two issues in my argument. However, both these issues are significant. Regarding commitment to and consensus on R2P, the contentious nature of this debate around humanitarian intervention has been discussed and it has been noted that much of the suspicion with which humanitarian intervention is approached has migrated into the attitudes of many states with regards to concerning R2P. Furthermore, the fact that the debates around humanitarian intervention and R2P have involved the issue of sovereignty and the norm of non-intervention has meant that this is a significant issue, and the inability of the U.S. and the U.K to drive and secure consensus on and commitment to the new principle as a result of their diminished credibility as norm carriers is significant, as it should be seen in this light. Secondly, with regards to the crisis in Darfur, this was an issue of global proportions especially following the genocide in Rwanda in 1994; the international community committed itself to the prevention of such scenarios in the future.[320] Although the U.S. may at some point have had reason for not supporting more direct and harsh measures against the government in Khartoum based on its own national security interests, as the crisis in Darfur worsened it realised the need for concrete action.[321] With regards to the crisis in Darfur then, and the fact that both the U.S. and U.K realized that it was unlikely that they would be able to take a leading role in building a consensus in the Security Council on action concerning a humanitarian crisis of epic proportions is therefore also significant, and the issues should also be seen in this light.

Although there was broad support for the just cause threshold being set high, the notion that the primary responsibility to protect lay with the host state, and against the idea the use of the veto should be voluntarily limited by the P-5, one major point of contention remained, namely the criteria that would serve to guide decision-making regarding the use of force.[322] A number of P-5 governments displayed scepticism from the outset, as at the Security Council's May 2002 annual retreat, where "the US rejected the idea of criteria to guide decision-making on the grounds that it would not bind itself in ways that might constrain its right to decide when and where to use force."[323] China too, was unconvinced regarding the

---

[320] Strauss, 130-1.
[321] Michael Clough, "Darfur: Whose Responsibility to Protect?" 7-8, accessed June 27, 2010, http://responsibilitytoprotect.org/files/HRW_Darfur-WhoseResponsibilitytoProtect.pdf
[322] Alex J. Bellamy, "Whither the Responsibility to Protect? Humanitarian Intervention and the 2005 World Summit," *Ethics and International Affairs* 20 (2006): 164.
[323] Bellamy, *Responsibility to Protect*, 67.

R2P and demanded that all questions pertaining to the "use of force...be deferred to the Security Council."[324] China's concern was shared by Russia, who argued that the United Nations was already "equipped to deal with humanitarian intervention, noting that, by countenancing unauthorised intervention, R2P risked undermining the UN Charter."[325] Although supporting the R2P, France and the U.K. (as well as the U.S.) also unequivocally rejected the prohibition on unauthorised intervention in all circumstances, yet they too expressed concern.[326] In particular, these two states were concerned that consensus on criteria would not necessarily result in the political will and consensus needed for "effective responses to humanitarian crises."[327]

Whereas a number of African governments, Kofi Annan, the HLP and of course the ICISS argued that the criteria were a vital element of the R2P package,[328] as well as an essential part of ensuring transparency in Security Council decision-making, the U.S., Russia and China all rejected criteria, albeit for significantly different reasons.[329] The United States, was of the opinion that, as mentioned above, "criteria would limit its freedom of action" and could potentially "reinforce the concept's prescriptive component."[330] It further rejected the criteria on the basis that it "could not offer precommitments to engage its military forces where it had no national interests,"[331] while Moscow and Beijing on the other hand, were collectively opposed to the criteria due to concerns about potential abuse thereof,[332] and were also worried that consensus regarding the criteria "might open the door to greater interventionism in the internal affairs of UN member-states."[333]

This problem experienced in the Security Council, was reinforced by the unwillingness of practically all states to acquiesce to what was, for the then Secretary-General, the ICISS, the HLP and the AU a vital component of the R2P, namely the "set of criteria addressing the legitimacy of using military force."[334] The General Assembly resolution, relatively separate from any follow up by the Security Council, "omitted any language on these principles, whether in a specific R2P context or more generally."[335] While the five criteria originally articulated by the ICISS had survived the preliminary debate, they stumbled at the last:

---

[324] Ibid.
[325] Ibid.
[326] Ibid.
[327] Ibid.
[328] Evans, *From Humanitarian Intervention*, 716.
[329] Bellamy, *Whither the Responsibility*, 165.
[330] Ibid.
[331] Bellamy, *Trojan Horse*, 36.
[332] Bellamy, *Whither the Responsibility*, 165.
[333] Wheeler and Egerton, 121.
[334] Evans, *From Humanitarian Intervention*, 716.
[335] Ibid.

"caught, in effect, in a pincer movement between, on the one hand, the hostility of the United States...and on the other, the hostility of a number of developing countries who argued, with more passion than intelligibility, that to have a set of principles purporting to limit the use of force to exceptional highly defensible cases was somehow to encourage it."[336]

This chapter has provided a discussion of the main events and arguments that have underpinned the debate in the evolution of the R2P. The chapter opened with a version of the R2P as it was endorsed at the 2005 World Summit, identifying the three core pillars on which the principle rests. The main differences between the R2P as advocated by the ICISS and the way it stands in the 2005 World Summit outcome document are also identified. From here the discussion shifted to the events and arguments which informed the R2P debate, focusing first on the war on terror and the 2003 war in Iraq. The argument made with regards to this was that based on the fact that the U.S. and its allies had attempted an ex post fact humanitarian justification for that war, as well as the way in which the war on terror had been carried out, had left many states deeply sceptical of the new .[337] The second section focused on the crisis in Darfur, and has asserted that it has influenced the debate in two ways – firstly, the use of the language of R2P has not bridged the gap between sovereignty and humanitarian intervention and as endorsed by the World Summit the ICISS test for when R2P is transferred to the international community has been replaced with a style of wording which allows the host state to maintain the primary responsibility to protect civilians, thus averting a breach of its sovereignty. Secondly, the debates about intervention in Darfur have shown that the war in Iraq has weakened the moral standing and has diminished to a considerable extent the credibility of the U.S. and U.K. as norm carriers, thus having a negative impact on their ability to build international commitment to and consensus on the R2P principle. This second point was also used to argue for the central claim which underlies this thesis, that because of the weakening of the moral standing and the diminished credibility of the U.S. and U.K., the international system is experiencing a changing in the authors of rules of the system. The final section is comparatively brief and addresses the problem of Security Council buy-in on the criteria guiding the use of military force. The reasons for each of the P-5 members rejecting the criteria were identified and discussed, and it was acknowledged that objection to the criteria was not limited to the P-5 of the Council, but extended to the wider community of states.

---

[336] Ibid, 716-7.
[337] Bellamy, *Trojan Horse*, 33; Grono, 623.

Chapter 5

The Responsibility to Protect principle was the product of work done by the ICISS – a commission created by the Canadian government in response to a challenge made by the then Secretary-General Kofi Annan in his 2000 millennium report.[338] The ICISS believes that its report has addressed the central issues of the debate around humanitarian intervention in the 1990s, namely just cause, right authority and the tension between intervention for the protection of human rights and sovereignty.[339] The Report has, however, sparked its own debate. The principle progressed from inception in 2001 to international endorsement remarkably fast, as it was widely embraced by the international community at the 2005 World Summit.[340] However, there are significant differences between the version of the R2P as articulated in the Report and the way in which the principle is framed in the 2005 World Summit outcome document.[341] A large portion of the literature on the evolution of the R2P focusses on the progression of the principle from the ICISS report, to the HLP report, the Secretary-General's report and ultimately the 2005 World Summit outcome document. It has been the aim here to provide a discussion of the main events and arguments that have influenced the evolution of the principle.

The conceptual background to humanitarian intervention which is provided in chapter one aimed to highlight an underlying theme in the debate around humanitarian intervention, namely, the contentious nature thereof. This is significant for any discussion that deals with the R2P as this suspicion regarding humanitarian intervention has migrated into the debate around R2P as well as the attitudes with which many states have approached the principle. This suspicion towards humanitarian intervention is in large part due to the tension inherent in the relationship between intervention for the protection of human rights and sovereignty,[342] and as is mentioned above, although the ICISS asserts that this relationship between intervention and sovereignty is complementary,[343] the crisis in Darfur shows that infusing the debates around it with the language of R2P has done little to reconcile this tension.[344] The first chapter and the first section of the second chapter, namely that which deals with the past failures, the Secretary-General's challenge and the establishment of the ICISS, are intended to serve as a baseline from which to provide an understanding of what informed the Secretary-General's

---

[338] Evans, *The Responsibility to Protect*, 38.
[339] Quinn, 7.
[340] Bannon, 1158-9.
[341] Bellamy, *The Problem of Military Intervention*, 623; Bellamy, *Responsibility to Protect*, 83.
[342] ICISS, *Research, Bibliography, Background*, 17.
[343] MacFarlane, Thielking and Weiss, 978; Quinn, 34.
[344] Bellamy, *Trojan Horse*, 51.

decision to issue this challenge. It is also intended to serve as a basis from which to judge the significance of the Report as well as the concepts and ideas it introduces.

Focusing on the ICISS and R2P is the central theme of the second chapter; however, the discussion only moves to the core principles and principles for military intervention of R2P after the discussion has centred on the past failures of humanitarian intervention, the establishment of the ICISS, the origins of the concept of sovereignty, and ICISS's incorporation of the work of Francis Deng. The core principles of the R2P, as well as its principles for military intervention, are stated as they are articulated in the Report, and some degree of discussion is provided with regards to some of the principles, but not others, with space constraints being the primary reason therefore. Within this chapter emphasis is placed on the manner in which the ICISS, by changing the terminology from humanitarian intervention to R2P, has effected a change in the debate on humanitarian intervention, and the ICISS contends that shifting the language of the debate is advantageous in at least four ways.

The final chapter is concerned with the main events and arguments that have influenced the evolution of the R2P, and the chapter starts by providing the version of R2P as it is articulated in the 2005 World Summit outcome document. Within this section the main differences between the ICISS articulation of the R2P and that endorsed by world leaders in 2005 are identified. With regards to the main events and arguments influencing the evolution as they are discussed here, these are the war on terror and the 2003 war in Iraq, the crisis in Darfur and the problem of Security Council buy-in. In terms of the first, the manner in which the war on terror has been waged and the ex post facto humanitarian justification for the war in Iraq by the U.S. and its allies have served to breed hostility and suspicion towards the R2P. Turning to the crisis in Darfur, this has firstly, as has been mentioned repeatedly, shown that the infusion of the intervention debate with the language of R2P has done little to reconcile the tension between humanitarian intervention and sovereignty. This allowed for arguments that the primary responsibility to protect has remained with the Sudanese government,[345] resulting in the 2005 World Summit outcome document omitting the Report's empirical test for the transfer of the R2P from the host government to the international society, instead framing it in a manner which forestalls an encroachment on the host state's sovereignty.

Secondly the crisis in Darfur has brought to light the negative effect of the Iraq war on the moral standing of the U.S. and the U.K., as well as the diminishing effect it' has had on both these states' credibility as norm carriers – ultimately affecting their ability to build international consensus on and commitment to the R2P principle. This point is used as the

---

[345] Bellamy, *Trojan Horse*, 52.

basis from which I have argued for the claim which has underpinned my reasoning for doing this thesis, namely, that the international system is experiencing a shift in the writers of the rules of the system – a shift away from the U.S. and the U.K. The final issue discussed here as one of the central events which has influenced the evolution of the R2P is the problem of Security Council buy-in. Focusing on the rejection by the P-5 of the criteria to guide the use of force, and providing the reasons as to why each of these states rejected the criteria, as well as the acknowledgement that the objection to these were not limited to the Security Council P-5, but was expressed by the wider international community, allows understanding as to why the 2005 World Summit outcome document completely omitted any reference to the ICISS criteria.[346] As endorsed by the international community, the R2P has been termed 'R2P-Lite',[347] and is unquestionably a watered-down version of that articulated by the ICISS.[348] Where the ICISS has aimed to provide a structural and moral framework to guide the international community's response to humanitarian crises,[349] the points discussed above have been the primary influences on the evolution of the R2P, an evolution which has resulted in a principle which, although it has been internationally embraced, lacks much of the substance which would have enabled a decisive response from the international society to situations where such action is needed most.[350]

---

[346] Evans, *From Humanitarian Intervention*, 717.
[347] Weiss, Humanitarian Intervention, 117.
[348] Badescu and Bergholm, 291.
[349] Quinn, 79.
[350] Weiss, Humanitarian Intervention, 118.

References

Annan, Kofi. *Millennium Report of the Secretary General of the United Nations* New York: United Nations Department of Public Information, 2000.

Badescu, Cristina G., and Linnea Bergholm. "The Responsibility to Protect and the Conflict in Darfur: The Big Let-Down." *Security Dialogue* 40 (2009): 287-309.

Banda, Maria. *The Responsibility to Protect: Moving the Agenda Forward.* Ottawa: United Nations Association in Canada, 2007.

Banon, Alicia. "The Responsibility to Protect: The U.N. World Summit and the Question of Unilateralism." *The Yale Law Journal* 115 (2006): 1157-1165.

Bellamy, Alex J. "Responsibility to Protect of Trojan Horse? The Crisis in Darfur and Humanitarian Intervention After Iraq." *Ethics and International Affairs* 19 (2005): 31-53.

Bellamy, Alex J. "Whither the Responsibility to Protect? Humanitarian Intervention and the 2005 World Summit." *Ethics and International Affairs* 20 (2006): 143-169.

Bellamy, Alex J. "The Responsibility to Protect and the Problem of Military Intervention." *International Affairs* 84 (2008): 615-639.

Bellamy, Alex J. *Responsibility to Protect*. Cambridge: Polity Press, 2009.

Bellamy, Alex J., and Nicholas J. Wheeler. "Humanitarian Intervention in World Politics." Accessed June 28, 2010. http://www.cadair.aber.ac.uk/dspace/bitstream/2160/1925/1/Wheeler,%2520Bellamy.pdf

Chandler, David. "The Responsibility to Protect? Imposing the 'Liberal Peace'." *International Peacekeeping* 11 (2004): 59-81.

Charney, Jonathan. "Editorial Comments: NATO's Kosovo Intervention – Anticipatory Humanitarian Intervention in Kosovo," *American Journal of International Law* 93

(1993):834, quoted in Ronli Sifris, "Operation Iraqi Freedom: United States v Iraq – The Legality of the War," *Melbourne Journal of International Law* 4 (2003): 31.

Clough, Michael. "Darfur: Whose Responsibility to Protect." Accessed June 27, 2010. http://responsibilitytoprotect.org/files/HRW_Darfur-WhoseResponsibilitytoProtect.pdf

D'Amato, Anthony. "There is No Norm of Intervention or Non-Intervention in International Law," *International Legal Theory* 7 (2001): 33-41.

Deng, Francis M. "The Impact of State Failure on Migration." *Mediterranean Quarterly* 15 (2004): 16-36.

Evans, Gareth. "When is it Right to Fight?" *Survival* 46 (2004): 59-82.

Evans, Gareth. "From Humanitarian Intervention to the Responsibility to Protect." *Wisconsin International Law Journal* 24 (2006): 703-722.

Evans, Gareth. *The Responsibility to Protect: Ending Mass Atrocity Crimes Once and For All.* Washington D.C.: The Brookings Institution, 2008.

Evans, Gareth and Mohamed Sahnoun. "The Responsibility to Protect." *Foreign Affairs* 81 (2002): 99-110.

Feil, Scott R. "Could 5,000 Peacekeepers Have Saved 500,000 Rwandans?: Early Intervention Reconsidered." *Institute for the Study of Diplomacy* III (1997): 1-5.

Feinstein, Lee and Anne-Marie Slaughter. "A Duty to Prevent." *Foreign Affairs* 83 (2004): 136-150.

Grono, Nick. "Darfur: The International Community's Failure to Protect." *African Affairs* 105 (2006): 621-631.

Heinze, Eric A. "Humanitarian Intervention and the War in Iraq: Norms, Discourse, and State Practice." *Parameters* (Spring 2006): 20-34.

International Commission on Intervention and State Sovereignty (ICISS). The Responsibility to Protect. Ottawa: International Development Research Centre, 2001.

International Commission on Intervention and State Sovereignty (ICISS). *The Responsibility to Protect: Research Bibliography, Background.* Ottawa: International Development Research Centre, 2001.

International Criminal Tribunal for the former Yugoslavia. "Facts About Srebrenica." Accessed October 9, 2010. http://www.icty.org/x/file/Outreach/view_from_hague/jit_srebrenica_en.pdf

Kurth, James. "Humanitarian Intervention After Iraq: Legal Ideal vs. Military Realities." *Orbis* (Winter 2005): 87-101.

Lanz, David. "Conflict Management and Opportunity Cost: The International Response to the Darfur Crisis." *FRIDE* (September 2008): 1-8.

Levitt, Jeremy I. "The Responsibility to Protect: A Beaver Without a Dam?" *Michigan Journal of International Law* 25 (2003-2004): 153-177.

Lillich, Richard. "Intervention to Protect Human Rights," *McGill Law Journal* 15 (1969): 205, quoted in Ronli Sifris, "Operation Iraqi Freedom: United States v Iraq – The Legality of the War," *Melbourne Journal of International Law* 4 (2003): 31.

Macfarlane, S. Neil, Caroline Thielking and Thomas G. Weiss. "The Responsibility to Protect: Is Anyone Interested in Humanitarian Intervention?" *Third World Quarterly* 25 (2004): 977-992.

Mamdani, Mahmood. "Responsibility to Protect or Right to Punish?" *Journal of Intervention and Statebuilding* 4 (2010): 53-67.

McGrew, Anthony. "Globalization and Global Politics." In *The Globalization of World Politics: An Introduction to International Relations*, 3rd ed., edited by John Baylis and Steve Smith. Oxford: Oxford University Press, 2005.

Molier, Gelijn. "Humanitarian Intervention and the Responsibility to Protect After 9/11." *Netherlands International Law Review* LIII (2006): 37-62.

Piiparinen, Tuoko. The Lessons of Darfur for the Future of Humanitarian Intervention." *Global Governance* 13 (2007): 365-390.

Quinn, D.O. "The Responsibility to Protect." M.A. diss., Canadian Forces College, 2007.

Roberts, Adam. "The United Nations and Humanitarian Intervention," *Humanitarian Intervention and International Relations* 90 (2004), quoted in Thomas G. Weiss, "R2P After 9/11 and the World Summit," *Wisconsin International Law Journal* 24 (2006): 750.

Report of the 43rd Conference on the United Nations of the Next Decade. Actualizing the Responsibility to Protect. Accessed, June 28, 2010. Accessed http://ssm.com/abstract=1576639

Report of the High-Level Panel on Threats, Challenges and Change. A *More Secure World: Our Shared Responsibility*. U.N. Doc. A/59/565 (2004). Accessed June 26, 2010. http://www.un.org/secureworld/report/pdf.

Report of the Secretary-General Pursuant to General Assembly Resolution 53/35. *The Fall of Srebrenica*. U.N. Doc. A/54/549 (November 15, 1999).

Report of the Secretary-General. *In Larger Freedon: Towards Development, Security and Human Rights for All*. U.N. Doc A/59/2005 (2005), accessed June 26, 2010, http://www.un.org/largerfreedom/contents.htm

Report of the Secretary General. *Implementing the Responsibility to Protect*. U.N. Doc. A/63/677 (12 January 2009).

Roth, Kenneth. "War in Iraq: Not a Humanitarian Intervention." Accessed June 28, 2010. http://www.unhcr.org/refworld/pdfid/402ba99f4.pdf

Roth, Kenneth. "Was the War in Iraq a Humanitarian Intervention?" *Journal of Military Ethics* 5 (2006): 84-92.

Sifris, Ronli. "Operation Iraqi Freedom: United States v Iraq – The Legality of the War." *Melbourne Journal of International Law* 4 (2003): 521-561.

Stahn, Carsten. "Responsibility to Protect: Political Rhetoric or Emerging Legal Norm?" *The American Journal of International Law* 101 (2007): 99-120.

Stowell, Ellery. *Intervention in International Law* (Washington, DC: J. Byrne, 1921), 53, quoted in International Commission on Intervention and State Sovereignty (ICISS), "*The Responsibility to Protect: Research Bibliography, Background* (Ottawa: International Development Research Centre, 2001), 17.

Strauss, Scott. "Darfur and the Genocide Debate." *Foreign Affairs* 84 (2005): 123-133.

Taylor, Paul and Devon Curtis. "The United Nations." In *The Globalization of World Politics: An Introduction to International Relations*, 3rd ed., edited by John Baylis and Steve Smith. Oxford: Oxford University Press, 2005.

Tesón, Fernando R. "Ending Tyranny in Iraq." *Ethics and International Affairs* 19 (2005): 1-20.

Thakur, Ramesh. "Iraq and the Responsibility to Protect." *Behind the Headlines* 62 (2004): 1-15.

Thakur, Ramesh. "A Shared Responsibility for a More Secure World," *Global Governance* II (2005): 284, quoted in Alex J. Bellamy, "The Responsibility to Protect and the Problem of Military Intervention," *International Affairs* 84 (2008): 625.

Vincent, R. J. *Nonintervention and International Order* (Princeton, NJ: Princeton University Press, 1974), 13, quoted in Nicholas J. Wheeler and Alex J. Bellamy, "Humanitarian Intervention in World Politics," In *The Globalization of World Politics: An Introduction to International Relations*, eds. John Baylis and Steve Smith (Oxford: Oxford University Press, 2005), 557.

The United Nations (U.N.). "Charter of the United Nations." Accessed October 2, 2010. http://www.un.org/en/documents/charter/preamble.shtml

The United Nations (U.N.). "Report of the Independent Inquiry into the Actions of the United Nations During the 1994 Genocide in Rwanda," U.N. Doc. S/1999/1257 (December 15, 1999).

United Nations General Assembly, '2005 Summit Outcome,' Resolution A/RES/60/1 (Sept. 20, 2005); available at www.un.org/summit2005/documents.html.

Weiss, Thomas G. "R2P After 9/11 and the World Summit." *Wisconsin International Law Journal* 24 (2006): 741-759.

Weiss, Thomas G. *Humanitarian Intervention*. Cambridge: Polity Press, 2007.

Wheeler, Nicholas J. And Alex J. Bellamy. "Humanitarian Intervention in World Politics." In *The Globalization of World Politics: An Introduction to International Relations*, 3rd ed., edited by John Baylis and Steve Smith. Oxford: Oxford University Press, 2005.

Wheeler, Nicholas J., and Frazer Egerton. "The Responsibility to Protect: 'Precious Commitment' or a Promise Unfulfilled?" *Global Responsibility to Protect* 1 (2009): 114-132.

Williams, Paul D., and Alex J. Bellamy. "The Responsibility to Protect and the Crisis in Darfur." *Security Dialogue* 35 (2005): 27-47.

Woods, Ngaire. "International Political Economy in an Age of Globalization." In *The Globalization of World Politics: An Introduction to International Relations*, 3rd ed., edited by John Baylis and Steve Smith. Oxford: Oxford University Press, 2005.